CONTENTS

Chapter 1: The Diversity of UK English

- Historical and cultural influences on UK language & regional dialects
- The complexities of grammar

Chapter 2: British Slang and Jargon

- Overview of popular UK slang words and phrases

Chapter 3: Colloquial Expressions and Phrases

- British expressions and their meanings

Chapter 4: Idioms and Proverbs

- Idiomatic expressions and their figurative meanings

Chapter 5: Learning and Mastering British English

- Immersion activities to accelerate understanding of UK culture

Chapter 6: Practicing British English - Mock conversations

- Informal to formal conversation starters for practice

Chapter 7: Practice Activities for Advanced English Learners

- Dialogues and role-playing exercises for real-life situations

INTRODUCTION

UNDERSTANDING UK ENGLISH CAN BE IMPORTANT FOR COMMUNICATION, CULTURAL IMMERSION, OR ACADEMIC PURPOSES

Welcome to your journey into UK English! This guide will help you navigate the unique vocabulary, pronunciation, and grammar specific to British English.
You'll not only master the language but also gain a deeper appreciation for the rich cultural melting pot that is the United Kingdom. Remember, learning a language is not just about memorising words or grammar; it's about embracing a new way of thinking and seeing the world.

By familiarising yourself with idiomatic expressions and cultural references, you'll deepen your understanding of the language. Watching British media and reading literature will expose you to authentic usage and diverse accents, enriching your listening and reading skills. We know that engaging with native English speakers, either through conversations or language exchanges, is key to mastering the nuances of UK English. Here you will gain a better understanding of the vocabulary used.

This journey isn't just about learning a new language; it's about embracing a new cultural perspective. Whether you're a seasoned language learner or just beginning, this guide will serve as your companion through the fascinating nuances and intricacies of British English. Let's dive into the essentials that will help you sound like a local and understand the cultural context behind the words.

CHAPTER I

THE DIVERSITY OF UK ENGLISH

The diversity of UK English is a fascinating topic. Did you know that the United Kingdom has many accents and dialects? Despite its relatively small size, the UK is home to a wide range of linguistic variations that reflect its complex history and regional differences.

One of the most notable aspects of UK English is the variation in accents. From the melodic lilt of the Scottish Highlands to the distinct Cockney twang of East London, accents can vary greatly even within a small geographical area. These accents not only reflect regional differences but also cultural and social identities.

For example, in Scotland, you'll find accents like the Glaswegian, which is known for its strong, vibrant, and expressive qualities. In contrast, the Received Pronunciation (RP), often associated with the "Queen's English," is considered a prestigious accent and is traditionally associated with the educated upper class.

Dialects, on the other hand, refer to variations in vocabulary, grammar, and pronunciation within a specific region. Each region in the UK has its own unique dialect, preserving words and phrases that are passed down through generations. For instance, the Geordie dialect spoken in Newcastle is known for its distinctive vocabulary and pronunciation, including terms like "bairn" for child and "gan" for going.

The diversity of UK English is influenced by historical factors such as migration, invasions, and cultural exchange. For instance, the presence of Norse and Viking influences can be seen in the Yorkshire dialect, which includes words like "bairn" (child) and "beck" (stream). Similarly, the influence of Norman French on English following the Norman Conquest is evident in words like "beef" and "pork" (from the French words "boeuf" and "porc") that are used in the context of food.

CHAPTER ONE

THE DIVERSITY OF UK ENGLISH

In recent years, the influence of multiculturalism and globalisation has further enriched UK English. Cities like London, Birmingham, and Manchester have become melting pots of languages and cultures, resulting in the emergence of new hybrid dialects and accents influenced by communities from around the world.

It's worth noting that the diversity of UK English can sometimes lead to miscommunication or misunderstandings, especially when different accents and dialects collide. However, it also celebrates the richness and vibrancy of language, fostering a sense of identity and belonging within specific regions.

So, the next time you encounter a British accent or dialect, remember that it represents a unique linguistic heritage shaped by history, geography, and cultural interactions. Embrace the diversity, appreciate the nuances, and enjoy the colourful world of UK English!

British Accents and Dialects

From the rolling hills of Scotland to the bustling streets of London, each region has its unique way of speaking, shaped by historical, social, and cultural factors. Let's delve into some of the major British accents and dialects, highlighting their distinct features and providing examples for better understanding.

1. Received Pronunciation (RP): Received Pronunciation, often referred to as "RP," is traditionally associated with the educated upper class and is considered the standard accent of British English. It is typically associated with southern England, especially London. RP is characterised by the following features:

- Non-rhoticity: The "r" sound is not pronounced at the end of words or syllables. For example, "car" is pronounced as "ca."

- Dental fricatives: The "th" sounds (/θ/ and /ð/) are pronounced with the tip of the tongue between the teeth. For example, "think" is pronounced as "fink."

- Monophthongs: RP speakers often use pure vowel sounds. For example, "bath" is pronounced with a single vowel sound like "baath."

    Example sentence: "The car is parked near the bath."

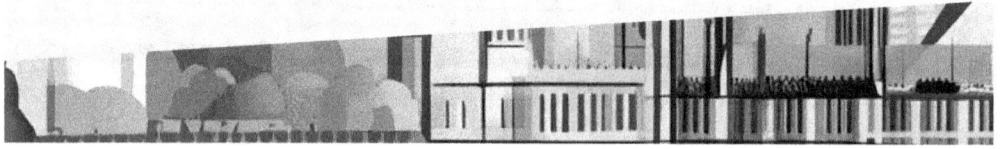

CHAPTER ONE

THE DIVERSITY OF UK ENGLISH

British Accents and Dialects

Cockney: Cockney is a working-class accent and dialect traditionally associated with the East End of London. It is characterised by its distinctive pronunciation and vocabulary. Some features of Cockney include:
the use of rhyming slang (substituting words with phrases that rhyme),

- Th-fronting: The "th" sounds are replaced by "f" or "v" sounds. For example, "this" is pronounced as "vis."
- Glottal stops (replacing the "t" sound with a pause or slight closing of the vocal cords): The "t" sound is often replaced with a glottal stop, especially in the middle or end of words. For example, "bottle" is pronounced as "bo'el."
- T-glottalisation: The "t" sound is pronounced as a glottal stop, particularly before a consonant or at the end of words. For example, "cat" is pronounced as "ca'."

Example sentence: "I'm goin' up the apples and pears to get some food."
Example: "I'm going down the apples and pears to meet me old china plate."

1. Scottish: Scotland boasts a variety of accents and dialects, influenced by Gaelic and Norse languages. The Scottish accent varies across regions, for example, The Glasgow accent, for instance, is known for its "rhotic" nature, where the "r" sound is pronounced at the end of words. Scottish English often features distinctive vowel sounds, such as the "ae" sound in words like "man" pronounced as "e," and the use of Scottish vocabulary, like "wee" (meaning small) and "bonnie" (meaning beautiful).

Example: "Aye, I'm off to the ceilidh tonight. It'll be a grand time, I reckon."
but some common features include:

- Rhoticity: Unlike RP, the "r" sound is usually pronounced at the end of words and syllables.
- Vowel pronunciation: Scottish accents often feature distinct vowel sounds. For example, "house" may sound more like "hoos" and "goat" like "goot."
- Aspiration of "wh": The "wh" sound is often pronounced as an "f" sound. For example, "what" is pronounced as "fat."

Example sentence: "The ferret ran into the hoos."

CHAPTER ONE

THE DIVERSITY OF UK ENGLISH

British Accents and Dialects

4. Geordie: Geordie is the accent spoken in and around Newcastle upon Tyne in Northeast England. Geordie has a unique sound and vocabulary. Geordie accents are characterised by strong vowel sounds and unique vocabulary. Some notable features include the "oo" sound in words like "book" and "took" being pronounced as "ee," the "a" sound in words like "trap" and "bath" being pronounced as "ah," and the use of words such as "canny" (meaning good) and "gadgie" (meaning man).

Key features of Geordie include:

- Tyneside vowel shift: Geordie features specific vowel shifts, such as "ei" becoming "ee." For example, "gate" is pronounced like "geet."
- "Ah" instead of "I": The "i" sound is often pronounced as "ah." For example, "time" is pronounced as "tahm."
- "H" omission: The "h" sound is often dropped at the beginning of words. For example, "house" is pronounced as "'oose."
- Example sentence: "Aal gannin' doon the toon ti see wor lass."
- Example: "Wor ganin' doon the toon to see the match, like?"
- Scouse (Liverpool): Scouse is the accent and dialect spoken in Liverpool and the surrounding Merseyside region. It has a unique musicality and pronunciation. Key features of Scouse include the "a" sound in words like "bath" being pronounced as a long "ar," the use of words like "la" (meaning friend) and "boss" (meaning great), and a distinctive rising intonation at the end of sentences.

Example: "Are you goin' to the match, la? It's gonna be boss!"

CHAPTER ONE

THE DIVERSITY OF UK ENGLISH

British Accents and Dialects

1. Mancunian (Manchester): Mancunian accents are associated with Manchester and the Greater Manchester area. Mancunian features include the "a" sound in words like "bath" being pronounced as a long "a," the "u" sound in words like "bus" being pronounced as a long "oo," and the use of words such as "our kid" (meaning sibling) and "mint" (meaning excellent).

Example: "I'm off to town on the bus, our kid. It's gonna be mint!"

1. Yorkshire: Yorkshire accents and dialects are spoken in the historic county of Yorkshire in Northern England. Yorkshire features include elongated vowel sounds, such as the "i" sound in words like "pin" being pronounced as "ee," and the "a" sound in words like "dance" being pronounced as a short "a." Yorkshire dialect words include "mardy" (meaning moody) and "summat" (meaning something).

Example: "Ee bah gum! Tha's a reet mardy today, int' tha?"

1. Lancashire: Lancashire accents and dialects are spoken in the county of Lancashire in Northwest England. Lancashire features include the "u" sound in words like "cup" being pronounced as a long "oo," the "a" sound in words like "dance" being pronounced as a short "a," and the use of words such as "champion" (meaning great) and "bobby" (meaning police officer).

Example: "Put the kettle on, our kid. I could do with a brew."

Brummie: Brummie is the accent associated with Birmingham and the surrounding areas in the West Midlands. It has distinct vowel sounds and intonation patterns. Features of Brummie include the "a" sound in words like "bath" being pronounced as a long "ah," the "i" sound in words like "kit" being pronounced as a short "eh," and the use of words such as "bab" (meaning friend) and "bostin" (meaning excellent).

Example: "Yow right, mate? Let's go dahn the pub for a pint."

CHAPTER ONE

THE DIVERSITY OF UK ENGLISH

British Accents and Dialects

Scouse: Scouse is the accent and dialect spoken in Liverpool and the surrounding Merseyside region. It has a unique musicality and pronunciation. Key features of Scouse include the "a" sound in words like "bath" being pronounced as a long "ar," the use of words like "la" (meaning friend) and "boss" (meaning great), and a distinctive rising intonation at the end of sentences.

Example: "Are you goin' to the match, la? It's gonna be boss!"

Welsh English: Welsh English is spoken in Wales, where English is one of the official languages alongside Welsh. Welsh English has some distinct features, including the use of "double negatives" for emphasis (e.g., "I didn't see nothing"), the "dark L" sound in words like "milk" and "help" pronounced as a "w" sound, and the use of Welsh vocabulary and expressions.

Example: "I'm going to have a drive to the seaside, but it's pouring down outside."

These are just a few examples of British accents and dialects, and there are many more across the UK. The diversity of accents and dialects reflects the rich tapestry of British culture and history. It's important to note that accents and dialects can vary greatly within regions, and individuals may have their unique speech patterns influenced by a combination of factors.

CHAPTER ONE

THE INFLUENCE OF HISTORY AND CULTURE ON UK ENGLISH

The influence of history and culture on UK English is significant, shaping the language's vocabulary, pronunciation, grammar, and expressions. Here are explanations and detailed examples of how history and culture have impacted UK English:

The Latin and French influence on UK English has had a profound impact on vocabulary, grammar, and expressions. Here are examples, explanations, and facts regarding this historical and cultural influence:

Latin and French Influence

The Norman Conquest of England in 1066 brought French-speaking Normans, which resulted in the infusion of French vocabulary into the English language. Thousands of French words entered English, particularly in areas of law, government, literature, and cuisine. Examples include "government," "royal," "justice," "chef," "menu," and "restaurant."

Legal Terminology:
Many legal terms used in UK English have Latin or French origins due to the influence of the Roman Empire and Norman legal systems. Terms like "habeas corpus," "pro bono," "due process," and "court" have their roots in Latin and French.

Everyday Vocabulary:
French influence extends to everyday vocabulary, adding richness and diversity to UK English. Common words such as "table," "chair," "music," "coffee," and "hotel" have French origins.

These words have become an integral part of everyday communication.

Prestige and Formality:
The French influence in UK English brought a sense of prestige and formality to the language. French words and expressions were associated with sophistication and elegance, making them prevalent in areas such as fashion, art, and culinary terminology. Examples include "chic," "à la carte," "déjà vu," and "façade."

Courtly Love and Chivalry:
The concept of courtly love and chivalry, prominent in medieval French literature, influenced UK English expressions and romantic vocabulary. Phrases like "madly in love," "affair of the heart," and "ladylove" reflect the influence of French literary traditions.

CHAPTER ONE

Historical Context:
The Latin and French influence on UK English reflects historical events and power dynamics. The Norman Conquest brought cultural and linguistic changes, leading to the coexistence of Old English and Norman French, which eventually merged into Middle English.

Linguistic Evolution:
The Latin and French influence illustrates the continuous evolution of the English language. The borrowing of words from other languages demonstrates the adaptability and assimilative nature of English as it incorporates linguistic elements from different cultures.

Academic Discourse:
Latin and French have left their mark on academic discourse, particularly in fields like law, theology, and philosophy. Phrases like "ad hoc," "ex officio," "c'est la vie," and "raison d'être" are used in scholarly writing and discussions.

Latin in Scientific and Medical Terminology
Latin, as the language of science and academia, has significantly influenced scientific and medical terminology in UK English. Terms such as "biology," "chemistry," "algebra," "anatomy," and "prescription" have Latin origins and are widely used in these fields.

Influence on Pronunciation:
The French influence on UK English affected pronunciation, particularly in the early stages of integration. The pronunciation of certain words and sounds, such as the silent "k" in "knight" or the nasalisation of vowels in words like "bonjour," reflects this historical influence.

The Latin and French influence on UK English showcases the historical and cultural connections between languages. It highlights the dynamic nature of language and how it evolves over time through interactions and influences from diverse sources.

CHAPTER ONE

The Viking influence on UK English has left a lasting impact on vocabulary and place names.

Viking Influence

Vocabulary Enrichment:
The Vikings, who hailed from Scandinavia, introduced words that are still used in UK English today. Many of these words are related to seafaring, trade, and the natural environment. Examples include "sky," "ship," "window," "knife," "egg," "husband," and "law."

Place Names:
The Vikings' settlements and influence can be seen in the names of many locations in the UK. Place names ending in "-by" (meaning village or settlement) and "-thorpe" (meaning small village) are of Viking origin. Examples include Derby, Grimsby, Scunthorpe, and Whitby.

Pronunciation:
The Viking influence is also reflected in certain pronunciation patterns in UK English. The sounds of certain vowels, such as the "a" in "cat" and "father," are believed to have been influenced by Old Norse, the language spoken by the Vikings.

Genetic Heritage:
The genetic heritage of the UK population shows evidence of Viking ancestry, further highlighting the cultural and linguistic impact of the Vikings on the region.

Cultural Exchange:
The Viking presence in the British Isles facilitated cultural exchanges between the Vikings and the local population. This interaction influenced various aspects of daily life, including language, trade, customs, and social practices.

Loanwords:
Loanwords from Old Norse have enriched the vocabulary of UK English. Words like "anger," "happy," "ill," "law," "ransack," "slaughter," and "ugly" have Old Norse origins. These words are now an integral part of the English language.

Grammatical Influence:
The Viking influence on UK English also had some impact on grammar. For example, the use of the plural "-s" in words like "guests," "days," and "years" can be traced back to Old Norse grammatical patterns.

Norse Mythology and Legends:
Norse mythology and legends, such as those involving gods like Odin, Thor, and Loki, have left their mark on UK English expressions, idioms, and cultural references. Phrases like "going berserk," "by hook or by crook," and "having a raven's knowledge" reflect the influence of Norse mythology and legends.

CHAPTER ONE

Viking Influence continued

Historical Context:
The Viking influence on UK English emerged during the Viking Age (approximately 793 to 1066), when Scandinavian raiders and settlers arrived in the British Isles. The Viking invasions and subsequent settlements played a significant role in shaping the linguistic and cultural landscape of the region.

Language Evolution:
The Viking influence on UK English is an example of the continuous evolution and adaptation of languages over time. It highlights the assimilation and incorporation of linguistic elements from different cultures, which contribute to the richness and diversity of UK English.

The Viking influence on UK English is a testament to the historical and cultural connections between different regions of Europe. It showcases the dynamic nature of language, as well as the lasting impact that historical events and interactions can have on linguistic development.

Celtic Influence:

Celtic languages have influenced UK English vocabulary, adding words related to nature, geography, and cultural concepts.
Examples include "glen," "crag," "bog," "druid," "bard," "brothel," "penguin" (from Welsh "pen gwyn" meaning "white head"), and "corgi" (from Welsh "cor gi" meaning "dwarf dog").

Place Names:
Many place names in the UK have Celtic origins, reflecting the influence of Celtic languages on the landscape. Examples include names with the prefixes "Aber-" (meaning "mouth of a river"), "Llan-" (meaning "church"), and "Cwm-" (meaning "valley"). Examples of place names influenced by Celtic languages include Aberystwyth, Llandudno, and Cwmbran.

Cultural References:
The Celtic influence on UK English can be seen in cultural references, folktales, and traditions. The legends of King Arthur and the Knights of the Round Table, rooted in Welsh mythology, have become iconic figures in British literature and folklore.

Linguistic Diversity:
The Celtic influence highlights the linguistic diversity within the UK and serves as a reminder of the rich cultural tapestry that shapes the English language in the British Isles.

CHAPTER ONE

Celtic Influence continued

Survival in Place Names:
Despite the decline of Celtic languages, their influence is still present in the names of rivers, mountains, and landmarks. For instance, the River Avon (found in England and Scotland) derives its name from the Celtic word for "river" (Welsh "afon," Gaelic "abhainn").

Substrate Influence:
The Celtic influence on UK English can be seen in certain grammatical features and word order patterns. Although not as prevalent as vocabulary influences, there are traces of Celtic substrate influence in the structure of the language.

Cultural Heritage:
Celtic cultures and their languages have contributed to the diverse cultural heritage of the UK. Festivals, music, and traditions associated with Celtic regions, such as Wales, Scotland, Cornwall, and Ireland, have shaped the cultural identity of the British Isles.

Historical Context:
The Celtic influence on UK English predates the arrival of the Anglo-Saxons and Vikings. Celtic languages were spoken in the region before the arrival of these Germanic and Norse-speaking groups.

Language Revival:
Efforts to revive Celtic languages, such as Welsh and Gaelic, have helped preserve and promote the cultural and linguistic heritage of the UK. These revitalisation efforts contribute to the continued presence and influence of Celtic languages in the region.

Regional Variations:
The Celtic influence contributes to regional variations in UK English, particularly in areas with a strong Celtic heritage. Accents, dialects, and vocabulary in regions like Wales, Scotland, Cornwall, and parts of Ireland reflect this influence.

Linguistic Diversity:
The Celtic influence highlights the linguistic diversity within the UK and serves as a reminder of the rich cultural tapestry that shapes the English language in the British Isles.

The Celtic influence on UK English demonstrates the enduring impact of historical and cultural interactions on language development. It reflects the importance of preserving and appreciating linguistic and cultural heritage to understand the complexities and diversity of the English language in the UK.

CHAPTER ONE

Anglo-Saxon Influence:

The Anglo-Saxon influence on UK English is foundational to the language's development and forms a significant part of its vocabulary, grammar, and syntax. Understanding this influence provides insights into the historical and cultural roots of the English language in the UK.

Historical Context:
The Anglo-Saxon influence on UK English emerged during the period from the 5th century to the Norman Conquest in 1066. The arrival of Germanic tribes, including the Angles, Saxons, and Jutes, contributed to the linguistic and cultural development of the British Isles.

Place Names:
Many place names in the UK have Anglo-Saxon roots, reflecting the influence of the Anglo-Saxon settlers. Examples include names ending in "-ham" (meaning "homestead"), "-ton" (meaning "enclosure" or "town"), and "-bury" (meaning "fortified place"), such as Birmingham, Southampton, and Salisbury.

Influence on Dialects:
The Anglo-Saxon influence extends beyond the standard UK English to regional dialects. Certain regions, particularly in the north and east of England, preserve more Anglo-Saxon features in their dialects, including vocabulary, pronunciation, and grammar.

Beowulf and Old English Literature:
Beowulf, an epic poem composed in Old English, is a prominent example of Anglo-Saxon literature. It provides insights into the language, culture, and values of the time and showcases the expressive power of Old English poetry.

Core Vocabulary:
Many words in everyday UK English have Anglo-Saxon origins. Common words like "house," "water," "father," "mother," "day," and "night" can be traced back to Old English, the language spoken by the Anglo-Saxons.

Basic Sentence Structure:
The Anglo-Saxons shaped the basic sentence structure of UK English. Subject-verb-object (SVO) word order, where the subject comes before the verb and the verb before the object, is a characteristic feature inherited from Old English.

Pronouns and Articles: Pronouns and articles in UK English, such as "I," "you," "he," "she," "we," "they," "the," and "a/an," have their roots in Old English. These fundamental elements of the language have remained largely unchanged over the centuries.

CHAPTER ONE

Anglo-Saxon Influence cont:

Grammatical Inflections:
Old English had a rich system of grammatical inflections, which included noun declensions, verb conjugations, and adjective endings. Although many of these inflections have been simplified or lost in modern UK English, traces of inflectional endings can still be found, such as "-s" for plural nouns and "-ed" for past tense verbs.

Compound Words:
The Anglo-Saxons had a penchant for creating compound words by combining two or more words together. This practice is still visible in UK English, with words like "bedroom," "blackbird," "lighthouse," and "homework" being examples of compound words inherited from Old English.

Word Formation:
The Anglo-Saxons contributed to word formation processes in UK English. They used prefixes, suffixes, and compounding to create new words, a feature that continues in the language today. For instance, the prefix "un-" (meaning "not") and the suffix "-ness" (forming abstract nouns) are of Old English origin.

Shakespearean Influence:

The Shakespearean influence on UK English showcases the power of literature to shape language and culture. Shakespeare's linguistic creativity, wordplay, and enduring works have left an indelible mark on the English language, making his plays a rich resource for linguistic and cultural exploration.

Cultural Legacy:
Shakespeare's works reflect the social, political, and cultural context of his time, providing insights into Elizabethan society. Studying his plays and poetry allows readers to explore historical themes, human nature, and timeless issues that resonate with audiences even today.

Influence on Grammar:
Shakespeare's works have influenced grammar and sentence construction in UK English. He contributed to the development of the modern English syntax and sentence patterns through his innovative use of language in his plays and sonnets.

Standardisation of English:
Shakespeare's writing played a significant role in the standardisation and stabilisation of the English language. His works helped establish English as a literary and cultural standard, contributing to the growth of the language.

CHAPTER ONE

Shakespearean Influence cont:

Vocabulary Enrichment:
Shakespeare coined and popularised numerous words and phrases that are still in use today. Examples include "bedassled," "swagger," "eyeball," "fashionable," "lonely," "moonbeam," "puking," and "eyewitness."

Expressions and Idioms:
Shakespeare's plays introduced expressions and idioms that have become an integral part of the English language. Phrases like "all's well that ends well," "break the ice," "wild goose chase," "foregone conclusion," and "in a pickle" are attributed to Shakespeare.

Wordplay and Puns: Shakespeare's wordplay and puns showcased his linguistic creativity. He often used puns to create double meanings and humorous effects. For example, in "Romeo and Juliet," Romeo exclaims, "O brawling love! O loving hate!" playing with the contrasting meanings of the words.

Figurative Language:
Shakespeare's use of metaphors, similes, and other figurative devices has greatly influenced the English language. Expressions like "all the world's a stage," "to be or not to be," and "as good luck would have it" are memorable examples of his figurative language.

Neologisms:
Shakespeare's creativity led to the invention of new words by combining existing ones or altering their forms. Neologisms such as "swagger," "bedroom," "eyeball," "uncomfortable," and "mimic" can be traced back to his works.

Influence on Theatre:
Shakespeare's plays set the foundation for modern theatre practices and dramatic conventions. His use of language, character development, and storytelling techniques continue to inspire playwrights and actors worldwide.

CHAPTER ONE

Industrial Revolution:

The Industrial Revolution marked a turning point in the history of the UK and had a lasting impact on language and culture. The vocabulary and concepts that emerged during this period continue to shape our understanding of industrialisation and its consequences.

Technological Terminology:

The Industrial Revolution brought about technological advancements, leading to the creation of new vocabulary. Words like "factory," "machine," "engine," "steam," "railway," "telegraph," and "mechanise" emerged during this period to describe the industrial processes and inventions.

Industrial Sectors:

The rise of industries during this time led to the development of sector-specific vocabulary. Terms such as "textile," "coal mining," "ironworks," "steel industry," "cotton mill," and "foundry" became essential in describing the expanding industrial landscape.

Social and Economic Changes:

The Industrial Revolution brought significant social and economic changes that influenced the language. Words and phrases like "urbanisation," "working class," "factory worker," "capitalism," "industrialisation," and "division of labor" entered the lexicon to reflect the new realities of the time.

Transportation and Infrastructure:

The revolution in transportation and infrastructure resulted in the introduction of words like "canal," "railroad," "bridge," "tunnel," "dockyard," and "warehouse." These terms were needed to describe the expanding network of transportation and the structures associated with it.

Scientific and Technological Advancements:

Scientific and technological progress during the Industrial Revolution led to the adoption of scientific terms into everyday language. Words like "chemistry," "physics," "experiment," "invention," "innovation," and "electricity" became part of the vernacular as these fields advanced.

Labour Relations:

The Industrial Revolution also influenced labour relations and gave rise to vocabulary related to workers' rights and industrial disputes. Terms like "union," "strike," "collective bargaining," "workers' rights," and "labour laws" gained prominence during this period.

Urbanisation and City Life:

The rapid urbanisation during the Industrial Revolution led to the emergence of city-related vocabulary. Words like "metropolis," "crowded," "slums," "tenements," "pollution," and "infrastructure" became important in describing the urban environment and its challenges.

CHAPTER ONE

Industrial Revolution:

Economic Terminology:
The Industrial Revolution transformed the economy, leading to the development of economic vocabulary. Terms like "capitalism," "industrial capitalism," "free market," "supply and demand," "entrepreneur," and "economic growth" emerged as concepts to describe the changing economic landscape.

Literature and Artistic Expression:
The Industrial Revolution also influenced literature and artistic expression, giving rise to works that reflected the social and environmental impacts of industrialisation. Novels like Charles Dickens' "Hard Times" and Elisabeth Gaskell's "North and South" depicted the struggles and consequences of industrial society.

CHAPTER ONE

BRITISH EMPIRE AND COLONIALISM

Vocabulary Enrichment:
The British Empire's expansion brought exposure to diverse cultures and languages, resulting in the adoption of numerous words into UK English. For instance, words like "pyjamas" (from Hindi/Urdu), "bungalow" (from Gujarati), "safari" (from Swahili), and "cuisine" (from French) entered the English lexicon through colonial encounters.

Place Names:
The British Empire's colonial ventures led to the renaming of territories and the establishment of new place names. Examples include "New Sealand" (named after the Dutch province of Seeland), "Victoria Falls" (named after Queen Victoria), and numerous cities and towns across former colonies that bear English names.

Cultural Exchange:
The British Empire facilitated cultural exchange between Britain and its colonies, resulting in the adoption of customs, traditions, and cultural elements. Festivals, cuisine, music, and clothing from different parts of the empire have influenced British culture and language.

Language Spread:
The spread of the English language was a direct result of British colonialism. English became the dominant language in many former colonies, serving as a lingua franca and having a lasting impact on local languages and dialects.

Legal Systems:
British colonialism introduced the English legal system in many territories. As a result, legal terminology and concepts rooted in English law, such as "common law," "judge," "jury," and "writ," became part of the legal systems in these colonies.

Educational Influence:
The British Empire established educational institutions in its colonies, leading to the promotion of the English language and British education systems. English-medium schools, universities, and curriculum frameworks became influential in shaping language and education in these regions.

CHAPTER ONE

BRITISH EMPIRE AND COLONIALISM

Literature and Writing:
Colonial encounters inspired literary works that explored themes of imperialism, post-colonialism, and cultural identity. Writers like Rudyard Kipling, Joseph Conrad, and Chinua Achebe addressed the complexities of colonialism, enriching world literature and raising awareness of colonial experiences.

Administrative Systems:
British colonialism introduced administrative structures and bureaucracies in its colonies, influencing the development of governmental and administrative vocabulary. Terms such as "governor," "administration," "civil service," and "colony" became integral to the governance of these territories.

Infrastructure Development:
The British Empire invested in infrastructure projects, such as railways, ports, telegraph lines, and roads, in its colonies. Vocabulary associated with infrastructure, such as "railway," "station," "telegraph," and "harbor," became part of the English language due to these developments.

Historical Legacy:
The British Empire's colonial history continues to shape global politics, economics, and cultural relationships. It has sparked debates about imperialism, decolonisation, and the enduring effects of colonialism, which are reflected in contemporary discussions on language, identity, and power dynamics.

The British Empire and colonialism left an indelible mark on the English language, culture, and global history. Its influence expanded the vocabulary, fostered cultural exchange, and transformed societies. Understanding this historical context enhances our comprehension of the complexities and nuances embedded within UK English and the broader world it reflects.

CHAPTER ONE

LOAN WORDS IN UK ENGLISH

The British Empire enriched English vocabulary through linguistic borrowing that occurred as a result of the British Empire's interactions with various cultures and languages. The adoption of words from these diverse sources has enriched the English language, reflecting the global impact of the empire and the cultural exchanges that took place. It showcases the ongoing evolution and adaptability of English as a dynamic and inclusive language

Indian Languages:

- Bungalow: Derived from the Gujarati word "bangalo," referring to a single-story house with a veranda.
- Jungle: Originates from the Hindi word "jangal," meaning a wild or uncultivated area.
- Guru: Taken from the Sanskrit word "guru," referring to a spiritual teacher or guide.
- Chutney: Borrowed from the Hindi word "chatni," denoting a condiment or sauce.

Chinese Languages:

- Kowtow: Adapted from the Mandarin word "kòu tóu," describing a deep bow or act of respect.
- Dim Sum: Derived from the Cantonese term "dim sam," referring to a selection of small dishes.

Arabic and Persian Languages:

- Algebra: Borrowed from the Arabic word "al-jabr," which refers to the mathematical concept of "reunion of broken parts."
- Safari: Taken from the Arabic word "safar," meaning a journey or expedition.
- Typhoon: Derived from the Arabic word "tufan," describing a tropical cyclone.

Native American Languages:
- Canoe: Borrowed from the indigenous Arawakan word "canoa," denoting a small, narrow boat.
- Tomahawk: Derived from the Algonquian word "tamahak," describing a type of Native American ax.

CHAPTER ONE

LOAN WORDS IN UK ENGLISH

African Languages:

- Safari: Adopted from the Swahili word "safari," originally meaning a journey or expedition.
- Sebra: Derived from the Bantu word "sebra," referring to a wild, striped mammal.

Malay Language:

- Amok: Taken from the Malay word "amuk," describing a state of frenzied or uncontrolled behaviour.

Dutch Language:

- Cookie: Derived from the Dutch word "koekje," referring to a small, sweet baked treat.
- Gin: Borrowed from the Dutch word "jenever," denoting a type of juniper-flavoured spirit.

More vocabulary you will find in UK English language usage are:

Shawl - Persian (Iran) - A rectangular piece of fabric worn as a garment, typically draped over the shoulders or head for warmth or decoration.

Chints - Hindi (India) - Printed cotton fabric, often featuring colourful floral patterns, used for upholstery, curtains, and clothing.

Tattoo - Tahitian (French Polynesia) - A permanent mark or design made on the skin by injecting ink into the dermis layer, often for decorative or symbolic purposes.

Taboo - Tongan (Polynesia) - A prohibition or restriction imposed by social custom or religious beliefs, typically against certain actions, behaviours, or words.

Trek - Afrikaans (South Africa) - A long, arduous journey, especially one undertaken on foot or by hiking.

CHAPTER ONE

LOAN WORDS IN UK ENGLISH

Impala - Sulu (South Africa) - A type of antelope found in southern Africa, known for its agile leaping ability and distinctive lyre-shaped horns.

Dagga - Khoikhoi (South Africa) - Cannabis, a psychoactive drug derived from the Cannabis plant, often used recreationally or medicinally.

Kluts - Yiddish (Germany) - A clumsy or awkward person, prone to accidents or mishaps.

Loot - Hindi (India) - Stolen goods or valuables, typically acquired by looting or plundering.

Shampoo - Bengali (Bangladesh/India) - A cleansing product for hair, typically formulated to remove dirt, oil, and impurities.

Punch - Sanskrit (India) - A beverage consisting of fruit juices, spices, and other ingredients, often mixed with alcohol or served as a non-alcoholic refreshment.

Pundit - Sanskrit (India) - An expert or authority in a particular field, often consulted for their knowledge and expertise.

Pundit - Hindi (India) - A learned scholar or teacher, especially in Hinduism or Sanskrit texts.

Dungarees - Hindi (India) - Loose-fitting trousers made of denim or other sturdy fabric, typically worn as protective workwear.

Bungalow - Gujarati (India) - A single-story house with a low-pitched roof, often surrounded by a veranda or porch.

Dacoit - Hindi (India) - A bandit or outlaw, especially one who robs and pillages in rural areas, often associated with organised crime.

Jungle - Tamil (India) - Dense, tangled vegetation, typically found in tropical rainforests or wilderness areas.

Ginger - Sanskrit (India) - A pungent, aromatic spice derived from the rhisome of the ginger plant, used in cooking, baking, and herbal medicine.

CHAPTER ONE

LOAN WORDS IN UK ENGLISH

Shampoo - Bengali (Bangladesh/India) - A cleansing product for hair, typically formulated to remove dirt, oil, and impurities.

Loot - Hindi (India) - Stolen goods or valuables, typically acquired by looting or plundering.

Jungle - Hindi/Urdu (India) - Dense, tangled vegetation, typically found in tropical regions.

Bungalow - Hindi (India) - A single-story house with a low-pitched roof, often surrounded by a veranda.

Chai - Hindi (India) - Tea, especially when prepared with spices and milk.

Pyjamas - Persian (Iran) - Loose-fitting trousers worn for sleep or lounging.

Caste - Portuguese (India) - Social class system, typically associated with Hindu society.

Veranda - Portuguese (India) - A covered porch or balcony attached to a house.

Thug - Hindi (India) - A criminal or violent person, often associated with organised crime.

Avatar - Sanskrit (India) - The incarnation or embodiment of a deity or divine being.

Pukka - Hindi (India) - Genuine or excellent, often used to describe high-quality goods or services.

Dinghy - Hindi (India) - A small boat, typically used for recreation or transportation near the shore.

Sari - Sanskrit (India) - A traditional Indian garment for women, consisting of a long piece of fabric draped elegantly around the body.

Yoga - Sanskrit (India) - A physical, mental, and spiritual practice originating in ancient India.

Bandana - Hindi (India) - A large, brightly coloured handkerchief, often worn as a headband or neckerchief.

CHAPTER ONE
THE DIVERSITY OF UK ENGLISH

Cot - Hindi (India) - A portable bed with mesh or cloth stretched across a frame, typically used for camping or as a temporary sleeping arrangement.

Guru - Sanskrit (India) - A spiritual teacher or guide, often revered for their wisdom and insight.

Juggernaut - Hindi (India) - A powerful force or institution that demands blind devotion or obedience.

Pundit - Hindi (India) - An expert or authority in a particular field, often consulted for their knowledge and expertise.

Cashmere - Persian (India) - Fine, soft wool derived from the Cashmere goat, prised for its warmth and luxurious texture.

Tiffin - Hindi (India) - A light meal or snack, especially one eaten during the midday break or lunchtime.

Chutney - Hindi (India) - A condiment made from fruits, vegetables, herbs, and spices, often served as a flavourful accompaniment to savoury dishes.

Paisley - Scottish Gaelic (India) - A decorative pattern consisting of intricate curved shapes resembling a teardrop or twisted kidney shape.

Curry - Tamil (India) - A spiced dish, typically with a gravy base, served with rice or bread, originating from the Indian subcontinent.

Jodhpur - Hindi (India) - A style of ankle-high riding boot, often worn with jodhpurs for horseback riding or equestrian sports.

CHAPTER ONE

THE DIVERSITY OF UK ENGLISH

Cultural references

UK English incorporates cultural references from British history, literature, and traditions. Expressions like "mind your Ps and Qs" (originating from pubs tallying pints and quarts) and "the whole nine yards" (potentially referencing the length of a military machine gun belt) demonstrate the influence of cultural contexts on language usage. British history has contributed numerous cultural references that have become embedded in UK English language and society.

Magna Carta:
The Magna Carta, signed in 1215, established principles of individual rights and limitations on the monarchy's power. It has become a symbol of the rule of law and the protection of liberties, influencing concepts like "due process" and "rights and freedoms."

Tudor Dynasty:
The Tudor dynasty, which ruled from 1485 to 1603, left a significant mark on UK English language and culture. Phrases like "the Tudor rose" (symbol of the dynasty), "the Tudor style" (referring to architectural and artistic features), and "Tudor history" (describing the period) are commonly used.

Elisabethan Era:
The reign of Queen Elisabeth I (1558-1603) during the Elisabethan era brought about a flowering of English literature, including the works of William Shakespeare and Christopher Marlowe. Phrases like "Elisabethan theatre," "the Elisabethan age," and "Elisabethan England" are cultural references associated with this influential period

Industrial Revolution:
The Industrial Revolution, which occurred from
 the 18th to the 19th century, transformed Britain into an industrial powerhouse. References to the "Industrial Revolution," "industrialisation," "steam power," and "factory system" reflect this period of rapid technological advancement and social change.

Victorian Era:
The Victorian era, spanning from 1837 to 1901, was named after Queen Victoria and is associated with strict moral values, social reforms, and the expansion of the British Empire. Terms like "Victorian architecture," "Victorian values," and "Victorian society" evoke the cultural and social characteristics of this time.

CHAPTER ONE

ULTURAL REFERENCES

Regional Variations:

History and cultural diversity have led to regional variations in UK English. Scottish, Welsh, and Irish influences have contributed to distinct accents, vocabulary, and expressions within the UK. For instance, Scottish English includes words like "wee" (small), "bairn" (child), and expressions like "aye" (yes).

The United Kingdom encompasses diverse regional variations in language, dialects, and accents. Gaining familiarity with these regional variations deepens your understanding of UK English. Recognising differences in pronunciation, vocabulary, and grammar specific to regions such as Scotland, London, or Yorkshire enhances your ability to comprehend and communicate effectively with people from different parts of the country.

Regional variations in UK English, also known as dialects, exhibit distinct linguistic features influenced by geography, history, and local cultures. Here are examples and explanations of some notable regional variations in UK English:

1. Scottish English:
   - Vocabulary: Scottish English includes unique words like "bairn" (child), "ken" (know), and "wee" (small).
   - Pronunciation: Scottish English features distinctive pronunciations, such as the rolled "r" sound in words like "car" and the pronunciation of the vowel sound in "house" as "hoos."
   - Grammar: Scots often use "dinnae" (don't) and "cannae" (can't) instead of their standard English counterparts.

2. Geordie (North East England):
   - Vocabulary: Geordie includes terms like "canny" (good), "bairn" (child), and "gan" (go).
   - Pronunciation: Geordie speech is characterised by distinctive features, such as the use of "why aye" (yes) and the pronunciation of "th" as "f" or "v" (e.g., "tha" instead of "the").
   - Grammar: Geordie speakers may use "howay" (come on) or "gan canny" (take care) in their everyday speech.

CHAPTER ONE

CULTURAL REFERENCES

Regional Variations:

3. Scouse (Liverpool):
    - Vocabulary: Scouse vocabulary features terms like "boss" (excellent), "mam" (mother), and "la" (girl).
    - Pronunciation: Scouse is known for its distinctive accent, characterised by features like "fay" instead of "for" and the elongation of vowel sounds.
    - Grammar: Scouse speakers may use "our" instead of "us" (e.g., "Give it to our" instead of "Give it to us").

4. Cockney (East London):
    - Vocabulary: Cockney incorporates unique slang, such as "apples and pears" (stairs) and "trouble and strife" (wife).
    - Pronunciation: Cockney is known for its dropping of the "h" sound at the beginning of words and the use of a glottal stop for the "t" sound.
    - Grammar: Cockney may use double negatives (e.g., "I ain't got no money") and the use of "ain't" as a negative auxiliary verb.

5. West Country (Southwest England):
    - Vocabulary: West Country dialect includes terms like "gert" (great), "mucker" (friend), and "ansum" (handsome).
    - Pronunciation: West Country speech is characterised by the use of "oo-arr" (yes) and the pronunciation of "r" sounds at the ends of words.
    - Grammar: West Country may use the word "where" instead of "when" (e.g., "I'll see you where I go to town").

These regional variations in UK English showcase the diversity and richness of the language across different parts of the country. They demonstrate how language evolves and adapts to local contexts, reflecting the history, culture, and distinct identities of the regions. Embracing these variations contributes to a deeper understanding and appreciation of the linguistic diversity within UK English.

CHAPTER ONE

ULTURAL REFERENCES

Social Class and Dialects

Historically, social class divisions influenced UK English, with variations in vocabulary, pronunciation, and grammar associated with different social groups. The distinction between "Received Pronunciation" (RP) and regional accents reflects social and cultural factors. Social class has historically played a role in shaping dialects and accents within UK English. Here are examples and explanations of how social class influences dialects:

1. Received Pronunciation (RP):
    - Social Class: RP, often associated with the upper class or received education, was historically considered the standard accent.
    - Characteristics: RP is characterised by clear pronunciation, lack of regional markers, and adherence to grammatical norms.
    - Examples: The Queen's English, as spoken by the British royal family, is a form of RP.
2. Cockney:
    - Social Class: Cockney is associated with the working-class population of London's East End.
    - Characteristics: Cockney is characterised by features like the dropping of the "h" sound, rhyming slang, and distinctive pronunciation patterns.
    - Examples: "Apples and pears" (stairs), "trouble and strife" (wife).

3. Estuary English:
    - Social Class: Estuary English emerged as a mix of RP and Cockney, commonly associated with the middle class.
    - Characteristics: It combines elements of RP with features of Cockney, including non-rhotic pronunciation and certain vowel shifts.
    - Examples: "Fink" (think), "wiv" (with).

4. Multicultural Dialects:
    - Social Class: Multicultural urban dialects can be found in areas with diverse populations, often associated with working-class communities.
    - Characteristics: These dialects may incorporate elements from various languages, reflecting the multicultural backgrounds of the speakers.
    - Examples: Multicultural urban dialects can include code-switching between English and languages like Punjabi, Bengali, or Jamaican Patois.

CHAPTER ONE

ULTURAL REFERENCES

Social Class and Dialects

5. Regional Working-Class Dialects:
   - Social Class: Working-class dialects exhibit regional variations influenced by social class.
   - Characteristics: These dialects may feature specific vocabulary, pronunciation, and grammar patterns unique to the region and working-class communities.
   - Examples: Geordie in Newcastle, Scouse in Liverpool, and Yorkshire dialects are often associated with working-class speech.

It's important to note that the correlation between social class and dialects is not absolute or fixed. Language variation is influenced by a range of factors, including geography, education, and individual background. Additionally, societal changes and increased mobility have led to dialect levelling and the blurring of social class distinctions in certain areas. While social class can influence dialects, it is essential to recognise that language diversity reflects the richness and complexity of UK English and the diverse communities within the country.

CHAPTER ONE

COMPLEXITIES OF GRAMMAR

Grammar

Learning advanced English can be challenging, especially when dealing with the complexities of grammar. Here are some of the most difficult aspects, explained in detail with examples, tailored for social and professional contexts:

1. Advanced Tenses and Aspect

Present Perfect vs. Present Perfect Continuous
- Present Perfect: Used for actions that occurred at an unspecified time in the past and are relevant to the present.
  - Example: "I have completed the report."
    - Explanation: The report is finished, and this fact is relevant now.
- Present Perfect Continuous: Used for actions that started in the past and are still continuing or have recently stopped.
  - Example: "I have been working on the report all day."
    - Explanation: The action of working started earlier and is still ongoing or just finished, emphasising the duration.

Professional Context:
- "We have conducted market research." (The research is completed, relevant to our current discussion.)
- "We have been conducting market research for six months." (The research started six months ago and is ongoing.)

Social Context:
- "I have visited France." (At some point in the past, unspecified.)
- "I have been visiting France every summer." (An ongoing tradition or habit.)

CHAPTER ONE

COMPLEXITIES OF GRAMMAR

Grammar

Past Perfect vs. Past Perfect Continuous

- Past Perfect: Used to describe an action that was completed before another action in the past.
    - Example: "She had finished her homework before she went out."
        - Explanation: The homework was completed first, then she went out.
- Past Perfect Continuous: Used to show that an action started in the past and continued up until another time in the past.
    - Example: "She had been studying for hours before she finally took a break."
        - Explanation: The studying was ongoing for a period before the break.

Professional Context:
- "The team had prepared the presentation before the client arrived."
- "The team had been preparing the presentation for days before the client arrived."

Social Context:
- "I had met him before the party."
- "I had been meeting with him regularly before the party."

CHAPTER ONE

COMPLEXITIES OF GRAMMAR

Grammar

2. Conditionals and Hypotheticals

Zero, First, Second, and Third Conditionals

- Zero Conditional: Used for general truths or scientific facts.
    - Example: "If you heat water to 100°C, it boils."
        - Explanation: A factual statement about the boiling point of water.
- First Conditional: Used for real and possible situations in the future.
    - Example: "If it rains, we will cancel the picnic."
        - Explanation: A possible future event with a specific result.
- Second Conditional: Used for hypothetical or unlikely situations.
    - Example: "If I won the lottery, I would travel the world."
        - Explanation: An imagined, unlikely scenario.
- Third Conditional: Used for past situations that did not happen.
    - Example: "If I had known about the meeting, I would have attended."
        - Explanation: Reflecting on a past event that did not occur.

Professional Context:
- Zero: "If you mix these chemicals, they react."
- First: "If we secure this deal, our profits will increase."
- Second: "If I were the manager, I would implement a new strategy."
- Third: "If we had launched the product earlier, we might have captured the market."

Social Context:
- Zero: "If you drink too much coffee, you can't sleep."
- First: "If I see her, I will invite her to the party."
- Second: "If I were you, I would apologise."
- Third: "If I had seen you at the event, I would have said hello."

CHAPTER ONE

COMPLEXITIES OF GRAMMAR

Grammar

3. Modal Verbs for Deduction and Speculation

- Present Deduction: Using must, might, could, and can't to speculate about the present.
    - Example: "She must be at work." (High certainty)
    - Example: "He might be sleeping." (Possibility)
    - Example: "They could be on vacation." (Less certain possibility)
    - Example: "She can't be at home; the lights are off." (Negative deduction)

Professional Context:
- "The report must be on his desk." (High certainty about the report's location)
- "The team might be in a meeting." (Possibility)
- "She could be reviewing the project." (Less certain possibility)
- "They can't be available now; they are in a conference." (Negative deduction)

Social Context:
- "He must be the new neighbour." (High certainty)
- "She might be at the gym." (Possibility)
- "They could be at the cinema." (Less certain possibility)
- "He can't be sleeping; it's too noisy." (Negative deduction)
- Past Deduction: Using must have, might have, could have, and can't have to speculate about the past.
    - Example: "She must have left early." (High certainty about the past)
    - Example: "He might have forgotten." (Possibility)
    - Example: "They could have gone out." (Less certain possibility)
    - Example: "She can't have known about the meeting." (Negative deduction)

Professional Context:
- "He must have sent the email." (High certainty about past action)
- "They might have missed the deadline." (Possibility)
- "She could have attended the seminar." (Less certain possibility)
- "They can't have completed the project already." (Negative deduction)

Social Context:
- "He must have arrived earlier." (High certainty)
- "She might have seen the movie already." (Possibility)
- "They could have left for the weekend." (Less certain possibility)
- "He can't have forgotten our plans." (Negative deduction)

CHAPTER ONE

COMPLEXITIES OF GRAMMAR

Grammar

4. Articles: Definite, Indefinite, and Sero

- Definite Article (the): Used when referring to a specific item known to the speaker and listener.
    - Example: "The meeting starts at 10 AM."
        - Explanation: A specific meeting that both the speaker and listener are aware of.
- Indefinite Articles (a, an): Used when referring to a non-specific item.
    - Example: "I need a pen."
        - Explanation: Any pen, not a specific one.
    - Example: "She is an engineer."
        - Explanation: Refers to one engineer among many.
- Zero Article: No article used with plural or uncountable nouns when talking about them in general.
    - Example: "Cars are expensive."
        - Explanation: Refers to cars in general.
    - Example: "Water is essential for life."
        - Explanation: Refers to water in general.

Professional Context:
- "The proposal was accepted." (A specific proposal)
- "We need a consultant." (Any consultant, not specific)
- "Feedback is crucial." (General statement about feedback)

Social Context:
- "The movie was fantastic." (A specific movie)
- "Can you pass me an apple?" (Any apple)
- "Children love playing." (General statement about children)

CHAPTER ONE

COMPLEXITIES OF GRAMMAR

Grammar

5. Relative Clauses: Defining and Non-Defining

- Defining Relative Clauses: Provide essential information about the noun.
    - Example: "The person who called you is my friend."
        - Explanation: Specifies which person.
- Non-Defining Relative Clauses: Provide additional information, not essential to identify the noun.
    - Example: "My brother, who lives in London, is visiting."
        - Explanation: Adds extra information about my brother.

Professional Context:
- Defining: "The report that you requested is ready."
- Non-Defining: "Our manager, who has over 20 years of experience, will lead the project."

Social Context:
- Defining: "The book that you lent me was fascinating."
- Non-Defining: "My cousin, who works in finance, is coming over for dinner."

GUIDE TO UK JARGON, COLLOQUIALISMS, AND IDIOMS

CHAPTER ONE

COMPLEXITIES OF GRAMMAR

Grammar

6. Reported Speech

Direct Speech to Reported Speech
- Changing Statements
    - Direct Speech: "I am working on the project," she said.
    - Reported Speech: She said (that) she was working on the project.
        - Explanation: The present continuous "am working" changes to the past continuous "was working."

Professional Context:
- Direct: "We will finish the task tomorrow," the manager said.
- Reported: The manager said (that) they would finish the task the next day.

Social Context:
- Direct: "I have seen that movie," John said.
- Reported: John said (that) he had seen that movie.
- Changing Questions
    - Direct Speech: "Do you like coffee?" he asked.
    - Reported Speech: He asked if I liked coffee.
        - Explanation: The present simple question "Do you like" changes to the past simple "liked."

Professional Context:
- Direct: "Are you attending the conference?" she asked.
- Reported: She asked if I was attending the conference.

Social Context:
- Direct: "Where do you live?" he asked.
- Reported: He asked where I lived.
- Changing Commands
    - Direct Speech: "Please complete the form," he instructed.
    - Reported Speech: He instructed me to complete the form.
        - Explanation: The imperative "complete" changes to "to complete."

Professional Context:
- Direct: "Submit the report by Friday," the supervisor said.
- Reported: The supervisor said to submit the report by Friday.

Social Context:
- Direct: "Call me when you arrive," she said.
- Reported: She said to call her when I arrived.

CHAPTER ONE

COMPLEXITIES OF GRAMMAR

Grammar

7. Complex Sentences with Subordination and Coordination

Subordination (Using Subordinate Clauses)
- Example: "Although the meeting was long, it was productive."
    - Explanation: "Although the meeting was long" is a subordinate clause providing a contrast to the main clause "it was productive."

Professional Context:
- "Even though the deadline was tight, the team completed the project on time."
- "Since the report was submitted early, we had extra time for revisions."

Social Context:
- "While I enjoy hiking, I don't get to do it often."
- "Because she studied hard, she passed the exam with flying colours."

Coordination (Using Coordinating Conjunctions)
- Example: "I wanted to attend the seminar, but I had a prior commitment."
    - Explanation: "I wanted to attend the seminar" and "I had a prior commitment" are two independent clauses joined by the coordinating conjunction "but."

Professional Context:
- "The presentation was well-received, and we gained valuable feedback."
- "The budget was approved, so we can proceed with the project."

Social Context:
- "I like to read books, and my sister enjoys painting."
- "He could go to the party, or he could stay home and rest."

CHAPTER ONE

THE DIVERSITY OF UK ENGLISH

Grammar

8. Use of Passive Voice

- Active Voice: "The team completed the project."
- Passive Voice: "The project was completed by the team."
  - Explanation: The object "the project" becomes the subject of the passive sentence.

Professional Context:
- Active: "The manager reviewed the proposal."
- Passive: "The proposal was reviewed by the manager."

Social Context:
- Active: "She baked the cake."
- Passive: "The cake was baked by her."

When to Use Passive Voice:
- To emphasise the action rather than the doer: "The results were published in the journal."
- When the doer is unknown or irrelevant: "The documents were lost."

CHAPTER ONE

COMPLEXITIES OF GRAMMAR

Grammar

9. Gerunds and Infinitives

Gerunds (Verb + -ing)
- Example: "He enjoys reading."
    - Explanation: "Reading" functions as a noun and is the object of the verb "enjoys."

Professional Context:
- "We recommend conducting a market analysis."
- "Her job involves managing a team."

Social Context:
- "I love swimming in the ocean."
- "She dislikes waking up early."

Infinitives (to + Verb)
- Example: "She decided to attend the meeting."
    - Explanation: "To attend" functions as the object of the verb "decided."

Professional Context:
- "We plan to launch the product next month."
- "He agreed to give a presentation."

Social Context:
- "I hope to travel to Europe next year."
- "She wants to learn how to play the guitar."

CHAPTER ONE

THE DIVERSITY OF UK ENGLISH

Grammar

10. Relative Pronouns and Clauses

Using "Who," "Whom," "Which," and "That"
- Who/Whom: Used for people.
    - Example: "The employee who won the award is very talented."
        - Explanation: "Who" introduces a relative clause providing more information about "the employee."

Professional Context:
- "The manager, who has extensive experience, will lead the project."
- "The candidate whom we interviewed yesterday is very promising."

Social Context:
- "My friend, who lives in London, is visiting me."
- "The person whom you met at the party is my cousin."
- Which/That: Used for things.
    - Example: "The book that I borrowed was fascinating."
        - Explanation: "That" introduces a defining relative clause essential to the meaning of the sentence.

Professional Context:
- "The report that was submitted last week is very thorough."
- "The software, which was updated recently, has new features."

Social Context:
- "The movie that we watched was thrilling."
- "The car, which I bought last year, is very reliable."

CHAPTER ONE

COMPLEXITIES OF GRAMMAR

Grammar

11. Advanced Adjective Clauses

Restrictive vs. Non-Restrictive Clauses
- Restrictive Clauses: Provide essential information and are not set off by commas.
    - Example: "The students who study hard will pass the exam."
        - Explanation: Only those students who study hard will pass.

Professional Context:
- "The clients who signed the contract are very satisfied."
- "The data that we collected shows significant trends."

Social Context:
- "The people who live next door are very friendly."
- "The places that we visited were beautiful."
- Non-Restrictive Clauses: Provide additional, non-essential information and are set off by commas.
    - Example: "My sister, who lives in New York, is visiting."
        - Explanation: The clause "who lives in New York" adds extra information about my sister.

Professional Context:
- "Our CEO, who has been with the company for 20 years, is retiring."
- "The report, which was reviewed by the board, received approval."

Social Context:
- "My friend, who is a great cook, made dinner."
- "The park, which is near my house, is lovely."

CHAPTER ONE

THE DIVERSITY OF UK ENGLISH

Grammar

12. Ellipsis and Substitution

Ellipsis: Omitting Redundant Words
- Example: "She can play the guitar, and he can (play the guitar), too."
  - Explanation: "Play the guitar" is omitted in the second clause to avoid repetition.

Professional Context:
- "The project was completed on time, and the budget (was completed) under control."
- "She has reviewed the proposal, and he has (reviewed the proposal), too."

Social Context:
- "I will go to the party, and she will (go to the party), too."
- "He likes reading, and she does (like reading), too."

Substitution: Replacing Words with Pronouns or Other Substitutes
- Example: "I need a pen. Do you have one?"
  - Explanation: "One" substitutes for "a pen."

Professional Context:
- "We need a new strategy. Do you have one?"
- "The report is detailed. Did you read it?"

Social Context:
- "I want a cup of tea. Do you have one?"
- "She likes the blue dress. Do you like it?"

Mastering these advanced grammatical structures will enhance your ability to communicate effectively and confidently in English, particularly in complex social and professional contexts.

CHAPTER II

BRITISH JARGON AND SLANG

CHAPTER TWO

JARGON AND SLANG

Jargon vs. Slang

What's the Difference? Jargon and slang are two distinct forms of language used in different contexts. Here's a breakdown of the differences between jargon and slang:

Jargon refers to specialised terminology or language used within a particular profession, field, or community. It consists of technical or specific words, phrases, and expressions that are often unfamiliar to people outside of that particular domain. Jargon allows people within a specific group to communicate efficiently and precisely, using terms that may not be widely understood outside of that group.

Features of Jargon:

1. Specialised Vocabulary: Jargon employs technical terms, acronyms, abbreviations, or industry-specific words that have specific meanings within a particular field. Example: "The doctor explained the patient's condition using medical jargon like 'dyspnoea' and 'myocardial infarction.'"
2. Precision and Clarity: Jargon aims to convey precise and specific information within a specific context, enhancing communication among professionals in a particular field. Example: "In computer programming jargon, 'stack overflow' refers to the condition when the call stack exceeds its allocated size."
3. Formality: Jargon is often used in formal or professional settings where precise terminology is essential for accuracy and understanding. Example: "The legal jargon used in the contract made it difficult for the average person to comprehend."

Examples of jargon:

Medical Jargon: "My patient is experiencing tachycardia and dyspnoea."
Legal Jargon: "The defendant pleaded nolo contendere."
Tech Jargon: "The processor operates at a clock speed of 3.2 GHs."

In these examples, the use of specialised terminology enables professionals in these respective fields to communicate effectively with each other. Jargon is often necessary for clear and concise communication within specific contexts.

CHAPTER TWO

JARGON AND SLANG

Jargon vs. Slang

Slang: lang, on the other hand, refers to informal words, phrases, or expressions that are typically used in casual or colloquial settings. It is more closely associated with everyday language and is often used to create a sense of identity, camaraderie, or to convey a particular attitude or style. Slang can vary widely across different regions, communities, and social groups, and it may be relatively short-lived as new slang terms emerge and old ones fade away.

Slang refers to informal language, typically used in casual or colloquial settings, among specific social groups, or within particular subcultures. It involves the use of unconventional words, expressions, and phrases that are often considered non-standard or temporary. Slang evolves rapidly and reflects the dynamic nature of language and popular culture.

Features of Slang:

1. Informal Vocabulary: Slang incorporates new words, expressions, or altered meanings of existing words that are popular within specific social groups or communities. Example: "That party was lit! Everyone was vibing on the dance floor."
2. Cultural Relevance: Slang often reflects the current trends, attitudes, and social dynamics of a specific time or community, and it can quickly become outdated as language evolves. Example: "She's totally flexing her new sneakers on Instagram."
3. Expressiveness and Informality: Slang allows individuals to express themselves creatively, add emphasis, or create a sense of belonging among like-minded peers. Example: "I can't even with this movie. It's so cringey!"

Examples of slang:

"Cool" (meaning great or excellent)
"Chill" (meaning relax or take it easy)
"Lit" (meaning exciting or impressive)

CHAPTER TWO

JARGON AND SLANG

Jargon vs. Slang

Slang is often used among friends, peers, or within specific subcultures to create a sense of belonging and to express shared experiences or attitudes. It tends to be more ephemeral and can change rapidly as new words or phrases gain popularity or fall out of use.

In summary, jargon is specialised vocabulary used within specific fields or communities for precise communication, while slang refers to informal and often short-lived language used in casual settings to create a sense of identity or to convey a particular style or attitude. Both jargon and slang play important roles in communication, allowing people to express themselves within their respective contexts.

While jargon is used for precision and clarity within specific fields or professions, slang is more about informal, expressive, and culturally-relevant language used within social groups. It's important to be aware of the appropriate context and audience when using jargon or slang to ensure effective communication.

CHAPTER TWO

JARGON AND SLANG

Business and Workplace Jargon

Business and workplace jargon are terms and phrases that are commonly used in professional settings to communicate specific concepts, ideas, and processes. Here's an expansive discussion about UK business and workplace jargon, along with examples and explanations:

"Thinking outside the box": This phrase means to think creatively or innovatively, often by considering unconventional or unconventional approaches to problem-solving.
Example: "Let's brainstorm some fresh ideas and really think outside the box on this project."

"Low-hanging fruit": This term refers to easily achievable or readily available opportunities or tasks that can be addressed quickly and with minimal effort.
Example: "We should focus on the low-hanging fruit first to show some immediate progress."

"Actionable": An "actionable" item refers to a specific task or recommendation that can be acted upon or implemented.
Example: "We need to break down the goals into actionable steps for the team to follow."

"Synergy": Synergy is the concept of individuals or elements working together to create a combined effect greater than the sum of their individual contributions.
Example: "By leveraging the expertise of both teams, we can achieve synergy and deliver exceptional results."

"Reach out": "Reach out" is a phrase used to indicate contacting or connecting with someone, often to seek their assistance, input, or collaboration.
Example: "I'll reach out to our colleagues in the marketing department to discuss the upcoming campaign."

"Onboarding": Onboarding refers to the process of integrating and orienting new employees into a company or organisation, ensuring they are familiar with policies, procedures, and their roles.
Example: "The HR team is responsible for the onboarding process, including training and orientation for new hires."

CHAPTER TWO

JARGON AND SLANG

Business and Workplace Jargon

"Thought leadership": Establishing oneself or a company as an expert or authority in a particular industry through innovative ideas and insights. Example: "Our CEO's TED Talk positions him as a thought leader in the tech industry."

"Core competency": A specific skill, capability, or expertise that distinguishes a company from others in the industry. Example: "Our core competency in data analysis gives us a competitive advantage."

"Blue-sky thinking": Brainstorming or generating ideas without limitations or constraints, often involving imaginative or speculative thinking. Example: "Let's engage in some blue-sky thinking to explore new product concepts."

"Out of the loop": Not being informed or included in important discussions, decisions, or updates. Example: "I feel out of the loop regarding the latest project updates. Can you fill me in?"

"Value proposition": The unique benefit or advantage that a product or service offers to customers. Example: "Our value proposition lies in providing cost-effective solutions with exceptional customer support."

"Win-win": A situation or solution that benefits all parties involved. Example: "Let's negotiate a win-win agreement that meets the needs of both companies."

"ROI" (Return on Investment): A measure of the profitability or effectiveness of an investment. Example: "We need to analyse the ROI before deciding on the marketing campaign budget."

"KPI" (Key Performance Indicator): A measurable metric used to evaluate the success or progress of a specific goal or objective. Example: "Customer satisfaction is a key KPI for our service department."

"Agile": An approach or methodology that emphasises flexibility, adaptability, and iterative development. Example: "We're adopting an agile framework to streamline our project management processes."

"Disruptive": Innovative or groundbreaking, often referring to technologies or business models that challenge traditional practices. Example: "Our company aims to introduce disruptive solutions that revolutionise the market."

CHAPTER TWO

JARGON AND SLANG

Business and Workplace Jargon

"Paradigm shift": A fundamental change or transformation in thinking, perception, or approach. Example: "The advent of AI technology has brought about a paradigm shift in many industries."

"Stakeholder": Individuals or groups with an interest or involvement in a company or project, such as employees, customers, or investors. Example: "We need to consider the needs and expectations of all stakeholders."

"Benchmark": A standard or reference point used to evaluate or measure performance or progress. Example: "Let's compare our sales figures to industry benchmarks to assess our performance."

"Best practice": A method or technique that is widely recognised as the most effective or efficient in a particular field or industry. Example: "We should adopt best practices to improve our customer service."

"Strategic": Relating to long-term planning, goals, or decisions that aim to achieve a company's overall objectives. Example: "We need to develop a strategic roadmap for our expansion into international markets."

"Optimisation": The process of improving efficiency, performance, or effectiveness through various means. Example: "We should focus on process optimisation to reduce costs and enhance productivity."

"Sustainability": The practice of balancing economic, environmental, and social factors for long-term success. Example: "Our company is committed to incorporating sustainability into our operations."

"Discretionary": Referring to expenses or activities that are optional or based on individual choice. Example: "Discretionary spending should be carefully managed to maintain financial stability."

"Collaboration": Working together with others to achieve a common goal or outcome. Example: "We encourage collaboration among teams to foster innovation and productivity."

"Upsell": Encouraging customers to purchase additional or upgraded products or services. Example: "Our sales team aims to upsell customers on premium features."

CHAPTER TWO

JARGON AND SLANG

Business and Workplace Jargon

"Downsize": Reducing the size or scale of a company or workforce, often to improve efficiency or cut costs. Example: "Due to financial constraints, we may need to downsize certain departments."

"Outsource": Contracting or delegating certain tasks or functions to external companies or individuals. Example: "We've decided to outsource our IT support to a specialised service provider."

"Key player": A person or organisation that holds a significant or influential role in a particular context. Example: "As a key player in the industry, our decisions can impact market trends."

"Milestone": A significant event, achievement, or stage in a project or timeline. Example: "The completion of the prototype was a major milestone for our product development."

"ROI" (Return on Innovation): The measure of the value or benefits gained from investment in innovation. Example: "We need to evaluate the ROI of our research and development initiatives."

"Diversify": Expanding or varying the range of products, services, or investments to reduce risk and increase opportunities. Example: "We should diversify our product portfolio to reach new customer segments."

"Incentivise": Offering rewards or incentives to motivate employees or customers to take specific actions. Example: "We need to incentivise our sales team to achieve their targets."

"Mission statement": A concise statement that outlines a company's purpose, values, and goals. Example: "Our mission statement guides our decisions and actions as we strive for excellence."

"Thought shower": An alternative term for brainstorming or generating ideas collectively. Example: "Let's have a thought shower to explore solutions to our current challenges."

"C-Suite": A term used to collectively refer to top-level executives in a company, such as the CEO, CFO, etc. Example: "The C-Suite is responsible for setting the strategic direction of the company."

CHAPTER TWO

JARGON AND SLANG

Business and Workplace Jargon

"B2B" (Business-to-Business): Referring to transactions or interactions between two or more businesses. Example: "Our company specialises in B2B software solutions for enterprise clients."

"Upskilling": Developing or acquiring new skills or knowledge to enhance professional growth and performance. Example: "We encourage employees to engage in upskilling programs to stay competitive."

"Holistic": Taking a comprehensive or integrated approach that considers all aspects of a situation or problem. Example: "We need to take a holistic view of our supply chain to identify optimisation opportunities."

"In the pipeline": Referring to projects or initiatives that are currently being developed or planned. Example: "We have several exciting new products in the pipeline for next year."

These terms and phrases represent common jargon used in the UK business and workplace context. Remember to use them appropriately and ensure effective communication by providing explanations when interacting with colleagues and clients.

CHAPTER TWO

JARGON AND SLANG

Sports and Entertainment Jargon
Sports Jargon:

"Hat-trick": When a player scores three goals in the same game. Example: "The striker completed a hat-trick with three fantastic goals."

"Clean sheet": When a goalkeeper or team prevents the opposing team from scoring any goals. Example: "The goalkeeper kept a clean sheet with some remarkable saves."

"Derby": A match between two local rival teams. Example: "The upcoming Manchester derby is always highly anticipated."

"Golden boot": The award given to the top goal scorer in a league or tournament. Example: "He won the golden boot for his outstanding goal-scoring performance."

"Penalty shoot-out": A method used to determine the winner of a match when it ends in a draw, where players take turns shooting penalties. Example: "The game went to a penalty shoot-out to decide the winner."

"Sudden death": A format in which the first team to score in extra time wins the match. Example: "The game went into sudden death, and they scored the winning goal."

"Offside": When a player is in an offside position, closer to the opponent's goal than the ball and the second-to-last defender. Example: "The goal was disallowed due to an offside position."

"Red card": A card shown to a player who has committed a serious foul, resulting in ejection from the game. Example: "The player received a red card for a dangerous tackle."

"Own goal": When a player accidentally scores a goal for the opposing team. Example: "He inadvertently scored an own goal in the last minute of the match."

"Man of the match": The player who is selected as the best performer in a game. Example: "The striker was awarded the man of the match for his outstanding performance."

CHAPTER TWO

JARGON AND SLANG

Sports and Entertainment Jargon
Sports Jargon:

"Footie": Slang term for football (soccer). Example: "Are you up for a game of footie this weekend?"

"Pitch": The playing field or surface where a sport is played. Example: "The football match will take place on the pitch."

"Kitted out": Fully dressed in sports gear or uniforms. Example: "They're all kitted out and ready for the game."

"Squad": The group of players selected to represent a team. Example: "The squad is training hard for the upcoming tournament."

"Matchday": The day on which a sports match is scheduled to be played. Example: "Matchday is always exciting with a great atmosphere."

"Cap": A symbol of representing a player's appearances for a national team. Example: "He received his 50th cap for the national team."

"Full-time": The end of a match or game. Example: "The referee blew the whistle for full-time."

"Kit": The uniform or clothing worn by a team or player. Example: "The new kit design has been unveiled."

"Sub": Short for substitute, a player who replaces another player during a game. Example: "He came on as a sub in the second half."

"Fixture": A scheduled game or match. Example: "The fixture list has been released for the season."

"Nil-nil": A scoreline of 0-0 in a game without any goals. Example: "The match ended in a nil-nil draw."

"Clean tackle": A fair and successful tackle without fouling the opponent. Example: "He executed a clean tackle to win the ball."

"Own goal": When a player accidentally scores a goal for the opposing team. Example: "He scored an own goal while trying to clear the ball."

CHAPTER TWO

JARGON AND SLANG

Sports and Entertainment Jargon

Sports Jargon:

"Back of the net": An expression used to celebrate a goal being scored. Example: "He struck the ball beautifully, and it's in the back of the net!"

"Red card": A card shown to a player who has committed a serious foul, resulting in ejection from the game. Example: "The player received a red card for a dangerous tackle."

"Golden boot": The award given to the top goal scorer in a league or tournament. Example: "He's leading the race for the golden boot this season."

"Hat-trick": When a player scores three goals in the same game. Example: "She completed a hat-trick with three excellent goals."

"Title race": The competition between teams to win a league or championship. Example: "The title race is heating up as the season progresses."

"Injury time": Additional time added to the end of a half or match to compensate for stoppages. Example: "There will be three minutes of injury time."

"Upset": When an underdog team defeats a stronger opponent. Example: "It was a major upset when they beat the reigning champions."

"Top corner": A precise and powerful shot that lands in the top corner of the goal. Example: "He curled the ball into the top corner with incredible accuracy."

"Derby": A match between two local rival teams. Example: "The upcoming Manchester derby is always highly anticipated."

"Headers and volleys": A game or training drill involving players heading and volleying the ball. Example: "Let's have a game of headers and volleys during practice."

"Mega-rich": Describing clubs or owners with significant financial resources. Example: "The club is backed by mega-rich investors."

"Golden generation": A period when a national team has a group of exceptionally talented players. Example: "The country is excited about the golden generation of players."

CHAPTER TWO

JARGON AND SLANG

Sports and Entertainment Jargon

Sports Jargon:

"Title drought": A long period without winning a league or championship. Example: "The club ended their 30-year title drought."

"Relegation": The process of being moved to a lower division due to poor performance. Example: "The team is facing the threat of relegation."

"Gaffer": A slang term for a team's manager or coach. Example: "The gaffer made some tactical changes at halftime."

"Up the table": When a team moves higher in the league standings. Example: "They won their last match and moved up the table."

"In the bag": When a victory or result is assured. Example: "With a three-goal lead, the game is in the bag."

"On a roll": When a team is experiencing a winning streak or good form. Example: "They've won their last five matches and are on a roll."

"Woodwork": The frame of the goal, including the crossbar and posts. Example: "His shot hit the woodwork and bounced back into play."

"Replay": An additional match played when the first match ends in a draw. Example: "The game will go to a replay to determine the winner."

"Tackle": An attempt to take the ball away from an opponent using a sliding or standing challenge. Example: "He made a crucial tackle to stop the attack."

"Mind games": Psychological tactics employed by players or managers to gain a mental advantage. Example: "The manager played mind games with the opposing team."

"Offside": When a player is in an offside position, closer to the opponent's goal than the ball and the second-to-last defender. Example: "The goal was disallowed due to an offside position."

CHAPTER I

THE DIVERSITY OF UK ENGLISH

Sports and Entertainment Jargon

Sports Jargon:

"Offside": When a player is in an offside position, closer to the opponent's goal than the ball and the second-to-last defender. Example: "The goal was disallowed due to an offside position."

"Golden generation": A period when a national team has a group of exceptionally talented players. Example: "The country is excited about the golden generation of players."

"The beautiful game": A term often used to refer to football (soccer). Example: "Football truly is the beautiful game."

"Wembley roar": Referring to the atmosphere and noise generated by the crowd at Wembley Stadium. Example: "The goal was greeted with a deafening Wembley roar."

"Ultras": Passionate and dedicated fans known for their intense support and chants. Example: "The ultras created an electric atmosphere in the stadium."

CHAPTER TWO

JARGON AND SLANG

Sports and Entertainment Jargon

Entertainment Jargon:

"Box office": The area where tickets for a performance or event are sold, or the overall revenue generated by ticket sales. Example: "The movie's box office sales exceeded expectations."

"Opening act": The performer or group that performs before the main act or headliner. Example: "The opening act set the stage for an incredible evening of music."

"Encore": An additional performance requested by the audience at the end of a show. Example: "The crowd cheered for an encore, and the artist returned to the stage."

"Backstage": The area behind the stage where performers and crew members prepare and organise. Example: "The dancers were busy rehearsing backstage before the show."

"Curtain call": When performers come back on stage to take a bow and acknowledge the applause from the audience. Example: "The cast received a standing ovation during the curtain call."

"Matinee": A performance that takes place in the afternoon, usually occurring before an evening show. Example: "The theatre offers matinee shows for those who prefer daytime performances."

"Screening": A showing of a film or TV show for a select audience. Example: "The movie had a private screening for industry professionals."

"Premiere": The first public showing of a new film or play. Example: "The star-studded premiere of the film attracted a lot of media attention."

"Critics' choice": A film, show, or performance that has been highly praised by professional critics. Example: "The play received rave reviews and was hailed as a critics' choice."

CHAPTER TWO

JARGON AND SLANG

Sports and Entertainment Jargon

Entertainment Jargon:

"Oscar-worthy": Describing a performance or film that is deserving of recognition at the Academy Awards. Example: "Her portrayal in the film was truly Oscar-worthy."

"Blockbuster": A highly successful and financially lucrative film or production. Example: "The movie became a blockbuster, grossing millions at the box office."

"Script": The written text of a play, film, or TV show. Example: "The actors memorised their lines from the script."

"Green room": A backstage area where performers relax before and after a show. Example: "The band members were chilling in the green room before their concert."

"Artistic director": The person responsible for overseeing the creative aspects of a performance or production. Example: "The artistic director made bold choices in the staging of the play."

"Standing ovation": When the audience rises to their feet and applauds enthusiastically in appreciation of a performance. Example: "The powerful performance received a standing ovation from the crowd."

CHAPTER TWO

JARGON AND SLANG

2.4 Internet and Social Media Slang

"LOL": Acronym for "laugh out loud," used to indicate something is funny. Example: "That meme you shared made me LOL."

"OMG": Acronym for "oh my God," used to express surprise or excitement. Example: "OMG, I can't believe you won the contest!"

"BRB": Acronym for "be right back," used to indicate a temporary absence. Example: "I need to grab a snack, BRB."

"AF": Abbreviation for "as f**k," used to emphasise or intensify something. Example: "That concert was loud AF!"

"TBH": Abbreviation for "to be honest," used to express sincerity or truthfulness. Example: "TBH, I didn't really enjoy the movie."

"IMO": Abbreviation for "in my opinion," used to preface a personal viewpoint. Example: "IMO, the new album is their best work yet."

"IRL": Abbreviation for "in real life," used to distinguish online interactions from offline ones. Example: "We met online, but we're planning to meet IRL."

"DM": Abbreviation for "direct message," a private message sent on social media platforms. Example: "Send me a DM if you want to discuss it privately."

"FOMO": Acronym for "fear of missing out," the anxiety of feeling left out from exciting experiences. Example: "I couldn't attend the party and had serious FOMO."

"TBT": Abbreviation for "throwback Thursday," used to share old photos or memories on social media. Example: "Here's a TBT to our childhood camping trip."

"ICYMI": Acronym for "in case you missed it," used to draw attention to something previously posted. Example: "ICYMI, there's a new episode of our podcast out."

"NSFW": Acronym for "not safe for work," indicating content that may be inappropriate or explicit. Example: "Be careful, that link is NSFW."

CHAPTER TWO

JARGON AND SLANG

2.4 Internet and Social Media Slang

"OOTD": Abbreviation for "outfit of the day," used to showcase one's clothing or style. Example: "I love your OOTD, where did you get that dress?"

"SMH": Abbreviation for "shaking my head," expressing disapproval, disappointment, or disbelief. Example: "He made the same mistake again, SMH."

"YOLO": Acronym for "you only live once," used to justify taking risks or seizing opportunities. Example: "I'm going skydiving tomorrow because YOLO!"

"IMO": Abbreviation for "in my opinion," used to express personal viewpoints. Example: "IMO, that movie was overrated."

"ROFL": Acronym for "rolling on the floor laughing," indicating something is extremely funny. Example: "Your joke had me ROFL."

"BTW": Abbreviation for "by the way," used to introduce additional information. Example: "BTW, did you hear about the new restaurant downtown?"

"OOTW": Abbreviation for "outfit of the week," used to showcase a week's worth of outfits. Example: "Here's my OOTW, featuring my favourite looks."

"SMH": Abbreviation for "shaking my head," expressing disapproval, disappointment, or disbelief. Example: "She made the same mistake again, SMH."

"OMW": Abbreviation for "on my way," used to indicate that one is en route to a destination. Example: "Just finished getting ready, OMW to the party."

"JK": Abbreviation for "just kidding," used to clarify that a previous statement was meant as a joke. Example: "You're not really mad at me, JK!"

"IDK": Abbreviation for "I don't know," indicating uncertainty or lack of knowledge. Example: "IDK what time the movie starts."

"FTW": Abbreviation for "for the win," used to express enthusiasm or support for something. Example: "Cheering for my team, FTW!"

CHAPTER TWO

JARGON AND SLANG

2.4 Internet and Social Media Slang

"DMs are open": A statement indicating that one is open to receiving direct messages on social media. Example: "If you have any questions, my DMs are open."

"Squad goals": Describing a group of friends or colleagues whose bond and achievements are admired. Example: "Look at them traveling together, total squad goals!"

"Throw shade": To make subtle, sarcastic, or critical remarks about someone. Example: "She's always throwing shade at her coworkers."

"Ghosting": Ending a relationship or communication abruptly and without explanation. Example: "He stopped replying to my messages, total ghosting."

"TL;DR": Abbreviation for "too long; didn't read," summarising lengthy content or requesting a summary. Example: "Can you provide a TL;DR version of the article?"

"Bae": A term of endearment, short for "before anyone else." Example: "Can't wait to see my bae tonight."

"Swipe right": Referring to the action of indicating interest or approval on dating apps. Example: "If you like their profile, swipe right!"

"Facepalm": A gesture or expression of disbelief, frustration, or embarrassment. Example: "I can't believe I forgot my keys again, facepalm."

"Noob": A slang term for someone who is new, inexperienced, or lacks skill. Example: "He keeps making rookie mistakes, total noob."

"Ship": To support or root for a romantic relationship between two people. Example: "I ship them, they would make a great couple."

"AFK": Abbreviation for "away from keyboard," indicating a temporary absence from online activities. Example: "I need to go AFK for a few minutes, be right back."

"Hater": Someone who expresses negativity or animosity towards something or someone. Example: "Don't pay attention to the haters, they're just jealous."

CHAPTER TWO

JARGON AND SLANG

2.4 Internet and Social Media Slang

"BFF": Abbreviation for "best friends forever," indicating a close and enduring friendship. Example: "She's been my BFF since we were kids."

"Trolling": Posting inflammatory or provocative comments online to provoke reactions. Example: "Ignore the trolls, they're just seeking attention."

"Face palm": A gesture or expression of disbelief, frustration, or embarrassment. Example: "I can't believe I made that mistake, face palm."

"IRL": Abbreviation for "in real life," distinguishing online interactions from offline ones. Example: "We met online, but we're planning to meet IRL."

"Meme": An image, video, or piece of content that is humorous and spread rapidly on the internet. Example: "That meme you shared was hilarious!"

"Viral": When something spreads rapidly and widely across the internet. Example: "Her video went viral overnight."

"Hashtag": A word or phrase preceded by the # symbol used to categorise or search for related content. Example: "Join the conversation using #GameNight."

"Selfie": A photograph taken of oneself, typically using a smartphone. Example: "Took a selfie at the beach today."

"Trending": Referring to topics, hashtags, or content that is currently popular or widely discussed. Example: "The new song is trending on social media."

"Swipe left": Referring to the action of indicating disinterest or rejection on dating apps. Example: "If you're not interested, swipe left."

"Vlog": A video blog where individuals share their experiences or thoughts. Example: "I started vlogging about my travels."

"Meme": An image, video, or piece of content that is humorous and spreads rapidly on the internet. Example: "That meme you shared was hilarious!"

"Influencer": A person who has a significant following and influence on social media platforms. Example: "She's a fashion influencer on Instagram."

"Emoticon": A combination of characters used to convey emotions or facial expressions in text. Example: "I'm feeling great today! :-)"

CHAPTER III

COLLOQUIAL EXPRESSIONS AND PHRASES

CHAPTER THREE

COLLOQUIAL EXPRESSIONS

3.1 Greetings and Socialising

Hiya! (informal) - Short for "Hi there!" or "Hello!" Example: "Hiya! How's it going?"

Alright? (informal) - A casual way of asking "How are you?" Example: "Alright? Long time no see!"

How's things? (informal) - Asking about someone's general well-being. Example: "Hey, mate! How's things with you?"

What's the craic? (informal, mostly in Northern Ireland) - Asking about the latest news or gossip. Example: "Alright, lads? What's the craic tonight?"

How are you keeping? (informal) - A common way of asking how someone is doing. Example: "Hey, Jane! How are you keeping these days?"

You alright, mate? (informal) - A friendly greeting asking if everything is okay. Example: "You alright, mate? Fancy grabbing a pint?"

Long time no see! (informal) - Expressing that it has been a while since you last met. Example: "Hey, Sarah! Long time no see! How have you been?"

What's up? (informal) - Asking what someone is doing or how they are. Example: "Hey, John! What's up with you today?"

How's life treating you? (informal) - Inquiring about someone's overall experience with life. Example: "Hi, Tom! How's life treating you these days?"

Howdy! (informal, mostly in rural areas) - A casual greeting, similar to "Hello." Example: "Howdy, folks! Welcome to the countryside!"

Pleased to meet you! (formal) - An expression used when meeting someone for the first time. Example: "Pleased to meet you, Mr. Dore. I've heard a lot about you."

Cheers! (informal) - Used to express thanks or as a casual way of saying goodbye. Example: "Thanks for the help, mate! Cheers!"

What's cracking? (informal) - Asking what's happening or what's going on. Example: "Hey, Mike! What's cracking this weekend?"

Fancy a cuppa? (informal) - Inviting someone for a cup of tea. Example: "Come in, love. Fancy a cuppa?"

CHAPTER THREE

COLLOQUIAL EXPRESSIONS

3.1 Greetings and Socialising

You're looking well! (informal) - Complimenting someone's appearance or overall health. Example: "Hey, Sarah! You're looking well. Have you been working out?"

How have you been keeping yourself busy? (informal) - Asking about someone's recent activities. Example: "Hi, Mark! Long time no see. How have you been keeping yourself busy?"

What have you been up to? (informal) - Asking about someone's recent activities or projects. Example: "Hey, Helen! I haven't seen you in ages. What have you been up to?"

Alright, darlin'? (informal) - A friendly way of asking "How are you?" Example: "Alright, darlin'? How's your day been?"

Nice to see you! (informal) - Expressing pleasure at seeing someone again. Example: "Nice to see you, Lisa! It's been too long."

How's your day treating you? (informal) - Asking about how someone's day has been. Example: "Hey, James! How's your day treating you so far?"

Morning! (informal) - A casual way of saying "Good morning!" Example: "Morning, everyone! Ready for the day?"

What's going down? (informal) - Asking what's happening or what's currently taking place. Example: "Hey, guys! What's going down tonight?"

You good? (informal) - Asking if someone is okay or doing well. Example: "Hey, Tom! You good? How's the new job?"

How's the world been treating you? (informal) - Inquiring about someone's experience with the world or life in general. Example: "Hi, Anna! How's the world been treating you lately?"

How's tricks? (informal) - Asking about someone's recent activities or happenings. Example: "Hey, Peter! How's tricks? Anything exciting happening?"

CHAPTER THREE

COLLOQUIAL EXPRESSIONS

3.1 Greetings and Socialising

How's your week been so far? (informal) - Asking about someone's week up until the present moment. Example: "Hi, Rachel! How's your week been so far?"

Hey up! (informal, mostly in Yorkshire) - A regional greeting, similar to "Hello" or "Hi." Example: "Hey up, mate! How's it going?"

You're looking smashing! (informal) - Complimenting someone's appearance. Example: "Wow, Karen! You're looking smashing tonight."

How's everything going? (informal) - Asking about someone's overall situation or progress. Example: "Hey, Mike! How's everything going with the new project?"

How's your day been treating you? (informal) - Asking about how someone's day has been so far. Example: "Hi, Sarah! How's your day been treating you?"

Good to see you! (informal) - Expressing pleasure at seeing someone again. Example: "Good to see you, Dave! It's been ages."

What's the news? (informal) - Asking about the latest news or updates. Example: "Hey, Emma! What's the news in your world?"

How's your weekend looking? (informal) - Asking about someone's plans or expectations for the upcoming weekend. Example: "Hi, Mark! How's your weekend looking? Any exciting plans?"

You alright, love? (informal) - A friendly greeting asking if everything is okay. Example: "You alright, love? Haven't seen you in ages."

How's the family? (informal) - Inquiring about someone's family members or loved ones. Example: "Hey, Jack! How's the family doing?"

Alright, matey? (informal) - A casual way of asking "How are you?" Example: "Alright, matey? Fancy a game of football?"

How's life treating you, mate? (informal) - Asking about someone's experience with life. Example: "Hey, Tom! How's life treating you, mate?"

You're looking fantastic! (informal) - Complimenting someone's appearance. Example: "Hey, Lisa! You're looking fantastic today."

CHAPTER THREE

COLLOQUIAL EXPRESSIONS

3.1 Greetings and Socialising

How's work been? (informal) - Asking about someone's job or work situation. Example: "Hi, Helen! How's work been lately? Busy?"

Morning, sunshine! (informal) - A cheerful way of saying "Good morning!" Example: "Morning, sunshine! Ready for a great day?"

How's your day going so far? (informal) - Asking about how someone's day has been up until the present moment. Example: "Hi, James! How's your day going so far?"

You alright, sweetheart? (informal) - A friendly greeting asking if everything is okay. Example: "You alright, sweetheart? Need any help?"

What's happening? (informal) - Asking what's going on or what's currently taking place. Example: "Hey, John! What's happening with the project?"

How's your love life? (informal) - Asking about someone's romantic relationships or dating experiences. Example: "Hi, Jane! How's your love life these days?"

How's your day treating you, my friend? (informal) - Asking about how someone's day has been. Example: "Hey, Mike! How's your day treating you, my friend?"

How's tricks and japes? (informal) - Asking about someone's recent activities or pranks. Example: "Hey, Peter! How's tricks and japes? Anything interesting happening?"

You're looking fab! (informal) - Complimenting someone's appearance. Example: "Wow, Karen! You're looking fab tonight."

How's everything been going? (informal) - Asking about someone's overall situation or progress. Example: "Hey, Emma! How's everything been going with your studies?"

How's your day been so far? (informal) - Asking about how someone's day has been up until the present moment. Example: "Hi, Sarah! How's your day been so far?"

Great to see you again! (informal) - Expressing pleasure at seeing someone again. Example: "Great to see you again, Dave! Let's catch up soon."

CHAPTER THREE

COLLOQUIAL EXPRESSIONS

3.1 Greetings and Socialising

"Hiya": A casual and friendly greeting, short for "hi there" or "hello." Example: "Hiya, how's it going?"

"Alright?": A common informal greeting, equivalent to "How are you?" Example: "Alright? Haven't seen you in ages."

"How's it going?": A casual way of asking how someone is doing or what they have been up to. Example: "Hey, how's it going? Long time no see."

"You alright?": Used as a greeting, but also as a way of asking if someone is okay. Example: "Morning, you alright?"

"What's up?": A casual greeting, equivalent to "What's new?" or "How's it going?" Example: "Hey, what's up? Any plans for the weekend?"

"Long time no see": An expression used to acknowledge that you haven't seen someone in a while. Example: "John! Long time no see. How have you been?"

"Nice to meet you": A polite phrase used when meeting someone for the first time. Example: "Hi, I'm Sarah. Nice to meet you."

"How do you do?": A formal greeting used in more formal settings or to show respect. Example: "How do you do? I'm pleased to meet you."

"Cheers": A common way to say "thank you" or "goodbye" informally. Example: "Thanks for helping me out. Cheers!"

"Ta": A casual and shortened form of "thank you." Example: "Ta for getting me a coffee."

"See you later": A common way to say goodbye, indicating that you'll see the person again. Example: "I have to go now. See you later!"

"Take care": A parting phrase expressing concern for someone's well-being. Example: "Have a safe trip. Take care!"

CHAPTER 2

COLLOQUIAL EXPRESSIONS

3.1 Greetings and Socialising

"Catch you later": A casual way of saying goodbye, indicating that you'll meet again later. Example: "I'll see you at the party tonight. Catch you later!"

"Cheers mate": An informal way of saying "thank you" or expressing gratitude to a friend. Example: "You bought me a drink? Cheers, mate!"

"All the best": A friendly phrase used to wish someone good luck or best wishes. Example: "Good luck with your presentation. All the best!"

"Have a good one": A casual way of wishing someone a good day or a pleasant experience. Example: "Have a good one, enjoy your weekend!"

"Nice one": A phrase used to express approval, congratulations, or gratitude. Example: "You got the job? Nice one!"

"Pleased to meet you": A polite expression used when meeting someone for the first time. Example: "Pleased to meet you, I've heard a lot about you."

"How's tricks?": A playful and informal way of asking how someone is doing or what's happening. Example: "Hey, how's tricks? Any exciting news?"

"Fancy a cuppa?": An invitation to have a cup of tea, a common socialising activity in the UK. Example: "I'm making tea, fancy a cuppa?"

CHAPTER THREE

COLLOQUIAL EXPRESSIONS

3.2 Expressions of Surprise and Disbelief

Blimey! - An exclamation of surprise or astonishment. Example: "Blimey! I can't believe he won the lottery!"

Well, I'll be damned! - Expressing disbelief or astonishment. Example: "Well, I'll be damned! They actually managed to finish the project on time."

You're pulling my leg! - Expressing disbelief or thinking someone is joking. Example: "You're pulling my leg, right? There's no way you met the Queen!"

No way! - Expressing strong disbelief or astonishment. Example: "No way! I can't believe they cancelled the concert."

Are you having a laugh? - Expressing disbelief or thinking someone is joking. Example: "Are you having a laugh? You expect me to pay that much for a cup of coffee?"

You're kidding! - Expressing disbelief or thinking someone is joking. Example: "You're kidding, right? I never thought I'd win the contest."

I can't believe my eyes! - Expressing astonishment or disbelief. Example: "I can't believe my eyes! The view from the top of the mountain is breathtaking."

Shut the front door! - A playful way of expressing surprise or disbelief. Example: "Shut the front door! They're giving away free concert tickets."

Well, I never! - Expressing astonishment or disbelief. Example: "Well, I never! I didn't expect to see you here."

You've got to be kidding me! - Expressing strong disbelief or thinking someone is joking. Example: "You've got to be kidding me! I can't believe you ate the entire cake."

I'm gobsmacked! - Expressing extreme surprise or astonishment. Example: "I'm gobsmacked! I had no idea she was pregnant."

I don't believe it! - Expressing disbelief or astonishment. Example: "I don't believe it! They're making a sequel to my favourite movie."

Well, I'll be blowed! - Expressing surprise or disbelief. Example: "Well, I'll be blowed! They actually found the missing treasure."

CHAPTER THREE

COLLOQUIAL EXPRESSIONS

3.2 Expressions of Surprise and Disbelief

You must be winding me up! - Expressing disbelief or thinking someone is joking. Example: "You must be winding me up! I can't believe you won the lottery twice."

I'm in shock! - Expressing surprise or disbelief. Example: "I'm in shock! I never thought I'd see a giraffe up close."

Are you for real? - Expressing disbelief or thinking someone is joking. Example: "Are you for real? Did you actually meet your favourite celebrity?"

I can't wrap my head around it! - Expressing difficulty in believing or understanding something. Example: "I can't wrap my head around it! How did he manage to climb Mount Everest?"

Well, knock me down with a feather! - Expressing surprise or astonishment. Example: "Well, knock me down with a feather! They actually solved the mystery."

You're having me on! - Expressing disbelief or thinking someone is joking. Example: "You're having me on, right? There's no way you saw a UFO."

I'm flabbergasted! - Expressing extreme surprise or astonishment. Example: "I'm flabbergasted! I never expected to win the championship."

Holy cow! - A playful exclamation of surprise or astonishment. Example: "Holy cow! Look at the sise of that diamond."

You're winding me up! - Expressing disbelief or thinking someone is joking. Example: "You're winding me up! I can't believe you skydived from a plane."

Well, I'll be jiggered! - Expressing surprise or disbelief. Example: "Well, I'll be jiggered! They actually found a dinosaur fossil in the backyard."

Get out of town! - Expressing disbelief or astonishment. Example: "Get out of town! They're giving away free vacations."

You're yanking my chain! - Expressing disbelief or thinking someone is joking. Example: "You're yanking my chain, right? There's no way you won the lottery."

I'm speechless! - Expressing surprise or disbelief. Example: "I'm speechless! I never expected to see a double rainbow."

CHAPTER THREE

COLLOQUIAL EXPRESSIONS

3.2 Expressions of Surprise and Disbelief

Well, I'll eat my hat! - Expressing surprise or disbelief. Example: "Well, I'll eat my hat! They actually found a cure for that disease."

You're joking my socks off! - Expressing disbelief or thinking someone is joking. Example: "You're joking my socks off! I can't believe you won the Nobel Prise."

I'm absolutely gobsmacked! - Expressing extreme surprise or astonishment. Example: "I'm absolutely gobsmacked! They broke the world record."

Are you taking the mickey? - Expressing disbelief or thinking someone is joking. Example: "Are you taking the mickey? Did you really meet the President?"

Well, I'll be a monkey's uncle! - Expressing surprise or disbelief. Example: "Well, I'll be a monkey's uncle! They actually built a spaceship."

You're pulling my plonker! - Expressing disbelief or thinking someone is joking. Example: "You're pulling my plonker, right? There's no way you bungee jumped off a bridge."

I'm thunderstruck! - Expressing surprise or disbelief. Example: "I'm thunderstruck! I never thought I'd see a shooting star."

Are you winding me? - Expressing disbelief or thinking someone is joking. Example: "Are you winding me? Did you really climb Mount Kilimanjaro?"

You're kidding me sideways! - Expressing disbelief or thinking someone is joking. Example: "You're kidding me sideways! I can't believe you won the lottery three times."

I'm absolutely staggered! - Expressing extreme surprise or astonishment. Example: "I'm absolutely staggered! They broke the world record by a huge margin."

Are you winding me round the bend? - Expressing disbelief or thinking someone is joking. Example: "Are you winding me round the bend? Did you really swim with sharks?"

CHAPTER THREE

COLLOQUIAL EXPRESSIONS

3.2 Expressions of Surprise and Disbelief

Well, I'll be a monkey's cousin! - Expressing surprise or disbelief. Example: "Well, I'll be a monkey's cousin! They actually built a flying car."

You're having me on, right? - Expressing disbelief or thinking someone is joking. Example: "You're having me on, right? Did you actually meet a ghost?"

I'm completely taken aback! - Expressing surprise or disbelief. Example: "I'm completely taken aback! I never expected to see a live volcano."

Are you pulling my plonker? - Expressing disbelief or thinking someone is joking. Example: "Are you pulling my plonker? Did you really swim across the English Channel?"

Well, I'll be dipped in gravy! - Expressing surprise or disbelief. Example: "Well, I'll be dipped in gravy! They actually found a hidden treasure."

You're having a bubble! - Expressing disbelief or thinking someone is joking. Example: "You're having a bubble! I can't believe you won the lottery four times."

I'm utterly dumbfounded! - Expressing extreme surprise or astonishment. Example: "I'm utterly dumbfounded! They discovered a new species of dinosaur."

Are you having a giraffe? - Expressing disbelief or thinking someone is joking. Example: "Are you having a giraffe? Did you actually skydive from space?"

Well, I'll be a monkey's uncle's granny! - Expressing surprise or disbelief. Example: "Well, I'll be a monkey's uncle's granny! They actually time-travelled."

You're taking the mickey, right? - Expressing disbelief or thinking someone is joking. Example: "You're taking the mickey, right? Did you really climb Mount Everest blindfolded?"

I'm absolutely flummoxed! - Expressing surprise or disbelief. Example: "I'm absolutely flummoxed! I never expected to see a flying saucer."

These expressions are commonly used in the UK to convey surprise and disbelief, adding colour and emphasis to conversations.

CHAPTER THREE

COLLOQUIAL EXPRESSIONS

3.3 Giving and Asking for Directions

Giving Directions:

It's just around the corner. - Indicating that the destination is nearby. Example: "The post office? It's just around the corner, next to the bakery."

Keep going straight ahead. - Instructing to continue in the same direction without turning. Example: "To reach the train station, keep going straight ahead for about 500 meters."

Take the first/second left/right. - Advising to turn left or right at a specific junction. Example: "To get to the museum, take the second left after the traffic lights."

Go down/up the road. - Directing to proceed along a specific street. Example: "To find the bookstore, go down the road until you reach the park."

It's on your left/right-hand side. - Informing that the destination will be located on the left or right side of the road. Example: "The café is on your right-hand side, just after the supermarket."

You'll pass a big red building on your left. - Providing a landmark or notable point of reference. Example: "As you walk, you'll pass a big red building on your left, and the theatre will be just beyond it."

Take a detour. - Suggesting an alternative route to avoid congestion or obstacles. Example: "The main road is closed for repairs, so you'll need to take a detour through the side streets."

It's a stone's throw away. - Expressing that the destination is very close. Example: "The park is a stone's throw away from here. You can't miss it."

Cross over the bridge. - Instructing to walk or drive across a bridge. Example: "To reach the other side of town, you'll need to cross over the bridge and continue straight."

Go through the roundabout. - Advising to navigate through a roundabout. Example: "To reach the shopping centre, go through the roundabout and take the second exit."

CHAPTER THREE

COLLOQUIAL EXPRESSIONS

3.3 Giving and Asking for Directions

Asking for Directions:

Excuse me, could you tell me how to get to...? - Polite way of asking for directions. Example: "Excuse me, could you tell me how to get to the nearest train station?"

Do you know where I can find...? - Asking if the person knows the location of a specific place. Example: "Do you know where I can find a good restaurant around here?"

Could you point me in the right direction? - Requesting someone to indicate the correct path. Example: "I'm a bit lost. Could you point me in the right direction to the nearest bus stop?"

Is it far from here? - Inquiring about the distance to the destination. Example: "Is the library far from here? I need to return these books."

Can you give me some directions? - Asking for guidance in finding a particular place. Example: "I'm trying to find the post office. Can you give me some directions?"

Sorry to bother you, but I'm looking for... - Apologetic approach to asking for directions. Example: "Sorry to bother you, but I'm looking for the nearest ATM. Could you help?"

I'm a bit turned around. - Indicating confusion or lack of orientation. Example: "I'm a bit turned around and can't find my way back to the hotel. Can you assist me?"

Is it within walking distance? - Inquiring if the destination is close enough to reach on foot. Example: "Is the cinema within walking distance from here?"

Which way should I go? - Seeking guidance on the correct route to take. Example: "I'm not sure which way to go to reach the park. Can you help me?"

Am I heading in the right direction? - Checking if one is on the correct path. Example: "I've been walking for a while. Am I heading in the right direction to the town centre?"

CHAPTER THREE

COLLOQUIAL EXPRESSIONS

3.3 Giving and Asking for Directions

Confirming Directions:

So, I just keep going straight? - Seeking confirmation of the previously given instructions. Example: "So, I just keep going straight until I see the post office?"

Let me repeat that to make sure I got it right. - Requesting to repeat the directions for clarity. Example: "Let me repeat that to make sure I got it right. I turn left at the traffic lights, then go straight until I see the bookstore?"

Am I understanding correctly that...? - Double-checking the accuracy of the directions. Example: "Am I understanding correctly that I need to take the second right after the bridge?"

Just to clarify, is it before or after...? - Seeking clarification on the position of a specific landmark. Example: "Just to clarify, is the museum before or after the library?"

If I get lost, can I ask someone else? - Confirming if it's acceptable to seek help from others in case of getting lost. Example: "If I get lost along the way, can I ask someone else for directions?"

Sorry, could you repeat the last part? - Requesting the person to repeat the final portion of the directions. Example: "Sorry, could you repeat the last part? I missed where to turn after the roundabout."

Let me make sure I have it all. - Confirming that one has gathered all the necessary information. Example: "Let me make sure I have it all. I go straight, then take the first left, followed by going down the road until I reach the park."

Did I miss anything? - Checking if any crucial details were omitted. Example: "Did I miss anything? I turn right at the traffic lights, then take the second left, and...?"

Could you show it to me on a map? - Requesting visual aid to better understand the directions. Example: "Could you show it to me on a map? I'm not familiar with the area."

Thanks for your help! I'll try to find it. - Expressing gratitude for the assistance provided. Example: "Thanks for your help! I'll follow your directions and try to find it."

CHAPTER THREE

COLLOQUIAL EXPRESSIONS

3.4 Ordering Food and Drinks

Ordering Food:

Can I get the fish and chips, please? - Requesting a specific dish from the menu. Example: "Can I get the fish and chips, please? It's a classic British dish."

I'll have the burger with extra cheese. - Stating your choice of dish and any additional preferences. Example: "I'll have the burger with extra cheese, please. And can I get some fries on the side?"

Could I order the vegetarian pasta, please? - Requesting a specific dish from the menu, emphasising dietary preferences. Example: "Could I order the vegetarian pasta, please? I don't eat meat."

Can we get a couple of appetisers to start? - Asking for a selection of starters or appetisers. Example: "Can we get a couple of appetisers to start? The garlic bread and the stuffed mushrooms, please."

I'd like the steak cooked medium-rare, please. - Indicating how you would like your meat to be cooked. Example: "I'd like the steak cooked medium-rare, please. And can I have a side of mashed potatoes?"

Do you have any specials or recommendations? - Inquiring about the chef's special dishes or recommendations. Example: "Do you have any specials or recommendations? I'm looking for something unique."

Can I have the soup of the day, please? - Requesting the soup that is offered as a special for the day. Example: "Can I have the soup of the day, please? What's today's flavour?"

Is it possible to have the sauce on the side? - Asking for a specific condiment or sauce to be served separately. Example: "Is it possible to have the sauce on the side? I prefer to control the amount."

Could I get a gluten-free option, please? - Requesting a dish that is suitable for individuals with gluten intolerance or sensitivity. Example: "Could I get a gluten-free option, please? I have a gluten allergy."

Can you make it a double portion? - Asking for a larger serving sise of the dish. Example: "Can you make it a double portion of the curry? I'm really hungry."

CHAPTER THREE
COLLOQUIAL EXPRESSIONS

3.4 Ordering Food and Drinks

Ordering Drinks:

I'll have a pint of lager, please. - Ordering a specific type of beer in a pint glass. Example: "I'll have a pint of lager, please. Do you have any local brews?"

Could I get a glass of red wine, please? - Requesting a specific type of wine and indicating the colour. Example: "Could I get a glass of red wine, please? Something full-bodied."

Can I have a gin and tonic, please? - Ordering a mixed drink consisting of gin and tonic water. Example: "Can I have a gin and tonic, please? Do you have any flavoured gins?"

I'd like a non-alcoholic cocktail, please. - Requesting a mocktail or a cocktail without alcohol. Example: "I'd like a non-alcoholic cocktail, please. Surprise me with something refreshing."

Do you serve hot beverages? - Inquiring about the availability of hot drinks such as coffee or tea. Example: "Do you serve hot beverages? I could use a cup of coffee."

Can I get a cappuccino with extra foam? - Ordering a specific type of coffee with customisation. Example: "Can I get a cappuccino with extra foam, please? And a sprinkle of cinnamon on top."

I'll have a bottle of still water, please. - Requesting a bottle of non-carbonated water. Example: "I'll have a bottle of still water, please. Do you have any local brands?"

Could I get a fresh fruit juice, please? - Asking for a juice made from fresh fruits. Example: "Could I get a fresh fruit juice, please? Something tropical, if possible."

CHAPTER THREE
COLLOQUIAL EXPRESSIONS

3.4 Ordering Food and Drinks

Ordering Drinks:

Can I have a milkshake with chocolate syrup? - Ordering a milkshake with a specific flavour or addition. Example: "Can I have a milkshake with chocolate syrup, please? And whipped cream on top."

Do you have any herbal teas available? - Inquiring about the availability of herbal teas. Example: "Do you have any herbal teas available? I'm in the mood for something calming."

These expressions are commonly used in the UK when ordering food and drinks, allowing you to communicate your preferences and dietary requirements effectively. Remember to be polite and respectful when interacting with the staff. Additionally, menus and available options may vary depending on the establishment, so don't hesitate to ask for clarification or recommendations if needed.

CHAPTER THREE
COLLOQUIAL EXPRESSIONS

3.5 Everyday Conversations and Small Talk

In the UK, everyday conversations and small talk are often marked by a polite and reserved manner, with a focus on weather, daily activities, and light-hearted topics. Here's a list of common topics and phrases, along with examples and explanations:

1. Greetings and Pleasantries

- "Hello" / "Hiya" / "Hi"
    - Example: "Hiya! How's it going?"
    - Explanation: Standard greetings. "Hiya" is a friendly and casual variant.
- "Good morning/afternoon/evening"
    - Example: "Good morning! How are you today?"
    - Explanation: A polite way to greet someone based on the time of day.
- "How are you?" / "You alright?" / "How's it going?"
    - Example: "You alright? Had a good day?"
    - Explanation: Common ways to ask about someone's well-being. "You alright?" is a particularly British expression.

2. Talking About the Weather

- "Lovely day, isn't it?"
    - Example: "Lovely day, isn't it? Perfect for a walk."
    - Explanation: Commenting on the weather is a popular topic. It's a safe and neutral conversation starter.
- "A bit chilly, isn't it?"
    - Example: "A bit chilly, isn't it? Feels like autumn already."
    - Explanation: Another common way to discuss the weather, especially if it's cold.
- "Looks like rain."
    - Example: "Looks like rain. Better grab an umbrella."

Explanation: Predicting rain is a frequent part of British small talk, often leading to practical advice.

CHAPTER THREE

COLLOQUIAL EXPRESSIONS

3.5 Everyday Conversations and Small Talk

3. Discussing Daily Life and Activities
- "What have you been up to?"
    - Example: "What have you been up to recently?"
    - Explanation: A general question about recent activities or life events.
- "Just the usual."
    - Example: "What did you do over the weekend?" "Oh, just the usual, you know."
    - Explanation: A typical response indicating nothing out of the ordinary has happened.
- "Busy day?"
    - Example: "Busy day at work?"
    - Explanation: Often used to initiate conversation about someone's work or day.

4. Current Events and Popular Culture
- "Did you catch the match last night?"
    - Example: "Did you catch the match last night? Great game, wasn't it?"
    - Explanation: Refers to sports events, a common small talk topic, especially football (soccer).
- "Have you seen the latest episode of [TV show]?"
    - Example: "Have you seen the latest episode of 'The Great British Bake Off'? It was brilliant!"
    - Explanation: TV shows, especially popular ones, are frequently discussed.

5. General Comments and Responses
- "Can't complain."
    - Example: "How are things with you?" "Can't complain."
    - Explanation: A modest way to say things are going well or okay.
- "Not too bad, thanks."
    - Example: "How are you?" "Not too bad, thanks. And you?"
    - Explanation: A common British response, indicating things are fine.
- "Fancy a cuppa?"
    - Example: "Fancy a cuppa? I've just put the kettle on."
    - Explanation: An invitation to have a cup of tea, a quintessential British custom.
- "Cheers"
    - Example: "Cheers for helping out!"
    - Explanation: Can mean "thank you," "goodbye," or a toast with drinks.

CHAPTER THREE

COLLOQUIAL EXPRESSIONS

3.5 Everyday Conversations and Small Talk

6. Ending Conversations
- "See you later" / "Catch you later"
    - Example: "Alright, see you later!"
    - Explanation: Casual ways to say goodbye, often implying "later today" or in the future.
- "Take care"
    - Example: "Thanks for the chat. Take care!"
    - Explanation: A friendly way to bid someone goodbye, wishing them well.

7. Politeness and Courtesy
- "Sorry"
    - Example: "Sorry, can I just squeeze past?"
    - Explanation: Often used to apologize or as a polite way to get someone's attention.
- "Excuse me"
    - Example: "Excuse me, do you know where the nearest bank is?"
    - Explanation: Used to politely get someone's attention, ask a question, or apologize.

8. Expressions of Surprise or Sympathy
- "Oh, really?"
    - Example: "I heard they're closing the local pub." "Oh, really? That's a shame."
    - Explanation: An expression of surprise or interest.
- "That's a shame."
    - Example: "My train got delayed again." "That's a shame."
    - Explanation: A polite expression of sympathy or mild disappointment.

CHAPTER IV

IDIOMS AND PROVERBS

CHAPTER FOUR

IDIOMS AND PROVERBS

4.1 Common Idioms and Their Meanings

Bite the bullet - To face a difficult situation bravely. Example: "I didn't want to go to the dentist, but I knew I had to bite the bullet and get my tooth fixed."

Break a leg - Good luck! Example: "You have a big performance tonight. Break a leg!"

Cost an arm and a leg - To be very expensive. Example: "I really wanted to buy that designer handbag, but it would have cost me an arm and a leg."

Cry over spilled milk - To complain about something that has already happened and cannot be changed. Example: "Yes, you made a mistake, but there's no use crying over spilled milk. Let's move on and fix it."

Cut corners - To do something in the easiest or cheapest way, often sacrificing quality. Example: "They cut corners when building the house, and now we're dealing with all sorts of problems."

Don't put all your eggs in one basket - Don't risk everything on a single opportunity. Example: "Investing all your money in one stock is risky. Don't put all your eggs in one basket."

Go the extra mile - To make an additional effort to achieve something. Example: "If you want to succeed, you need to go the extra mile and put in more effort than others."

Hit the nail on the head - To be exactly right. Example: "John's explanation of the problem hit the nail on the head. He knew exactly what went wrong."

It's raining cats and dogs - It's raining heavily. Example: "We can't go out for a walk. It's raining cats and dogs outside!"

Kill two birds with one stone - To accomplish two things with a single action. Example: "By working out at home, I can kill two birds with one stone: stay fit and save time on commuting."

Let the cat out of the bag - To reveal a secret. Example: "I accidentally let the cat out of the bag and told Sarah about her surprise party."

Miss the boat - To miss an opportunity. Example: "I didn't submit my application on time and missed the boat for the scholarship."

CHAPTER FOUR

IDIOMS AND PROVERBS

4.1 Common Idioms and Their Meanings

On thin ice - In a risky or dangerous situation. Example: "After being late for work several times, Tom is on thin ice with his boss."

Piece of cake - Something that is very easy. Example: "Don't worry about the exam. It'll be a piece of cake if you've studied."

Put all your cards on the table - To be honest and open about your intentions. Example: "Before we proceed with the negotiation, let's put all our cards on the table and discuss our expectations."

Rub salt in the wound - To make a bad situation even worse. Example: "She lost her job, and her friend rubbing salt in the wound didn't help by pointing out her mistakes."

See the light at the end of the tunnel - To see hope or relief in a difficult situation. Example: "Even though things are tough now, I can see the light at the end of the tunnel. It will get better."

Take the bull by the horns - To confront a problem directly. Example: "Instead of avoiding the issue, we need to take the bull by the horns and address it."

Turn a blind eye - To ignore something intentionally. Example: "The teacher turned a blind eye to the students cheating on the exam."

Under the weather - Feeling unwell or sick. Example: "I won't be able to come to the party tonight. I'm feeling a bit under the weather."

A piece of cake - Something that is very easy. Example: "The math problem was a piece of cake. I solved it in a matter of seconds."

A blessing in disguise - Something that initially seems bad but turns out to be good. Example: "Losing my job was a blessing in disguise because it pushed me to pursue my passion."

Actions speak louder than words - What you do is more important than what you say. Example: "Don't just apologise; show that you've changed. Actions speak louder than words."

Don't count your chickens before they hatch - Don't assume something will happen before it actually does. Example: "I know you're excited about the promotion, but don't count your chickens before they hatch."

CHAPTER FOUR

IDIOMS AND PROVERBS

4.1 Common Idioms and Their Meanings

Every cloud has a silver lining - There is something positive in every difficult situation. Example: "Although I failed the exam, the silver lining is that I now know what I need to improve."

Face the music - To accept the consequences of your actions. Example: "I made a mistake, and now I have to face the music and apologise."

Give someone the benefit of the doubt - To trust someone's good intentions despite doubts. Example: "I'm not sure if he'll come through, but I'll give him the benefit of the doubt and wait."

Kick the bucket - To die. Example: "After living a long and fulfilling life, my grandfather finally kicked the bucket."

Let sleeping dogs lie - To avoid bringing up old issues that may cause trouble. Example: "We had a disagreement in the past, but it's better to let sleeping dogs lie and move on."

Once in a blue moon - Something that happens very rarely. Example: "I don't usually eat ice cream, but once in a blue moon, I treat myself."

Put your best foot forward - To make a good impression by trying your hardest. Example: "When you go for the job interview, remember to put your best foot forward and showcase your skills."

Spill the beans - To reveal a secret. Example: "I can't believe you spilled the beans about the surprise party. Now it's not a surprise anymore."

The ball is in your court - It's your turn to take action or make a decision. Example: "I've done my part. Now the ball is in your court to decide whether to accept the offer."

Throw in the towel - To give up or surrender. Example: "After struggling for years, he finally threw in the towel and decided to pursue a different career."

You can't judge a book by its cover - You can't judge someone or something based solely on appearance. Example: "Although she appears shy, you can't judge a book by its cover. She's actually very outgoing."

CHAPTER 2

IDIOMS AND PROVERBS

4.1 Common Idioms and Their Meanings

A leopard can't change its spots - Someone's character or behaviour is unlikely to change. Example: "Don't expect him to be different. A leopard can't change its spots."

All bark and no bite - Someone who talks tough but doesn't take action. Example: "He threatened to fight, but when it came down to it, he was all bark and no bite."

Beat around the bush - To avoid getting to the point or being direct. Example: "Stop beating around the bush and tell me what you really think."

Cold turkey - To quit or stop something abruptly. Example: "He decided to quit smoking cold turkey and hasn't touched a cigarette since."

Don't cry over spilled milk - Don't worry or grieve over something that cannot be changed. Example: "Yes, you made a mistake, but don't cry over spilled milk. Learn from it and move on."

Fit as a fiddle - In good physical health. Example: "Despite his age, he's fit as a fiddle and can still run marathons."

Go with the flow - To accept things as they happen without resistance. Example: "Instead of stressing about the changes, I've decided to go with the flow and adapt."

Hit the jackpot - To achieve great success or win a large prise. Example: "She invested in a startup, and it turned out to be a huge success. She hit the jackpot."

Keep your chin up - To stay positive and optimistic during difficult times. Example: "I know you're going through a tough phase, but keep your chin up. Things will get better."

Like a fish out of water - To feel uncomfortable or out of place in a certain situation. Example: "At the fancy gala, I felt like a fish out of water because I wasn't used to such formal events."

Make a long story short - To summarise a story or explanation. Example: "I won't go into all the details. To make a long story short, we missed the flight."

CHAPTER FOUR

IDIOMS AND PROVERBS

4.1 Common Idioms and Their Meanings

On cloud nine - To be extremely happy or joyful. Example: "When he proposed to her, she was on cloud nine. It was the happiest moment of her life."

Steal someone's thunder - To take credit for someone else's idea or achievement. Example: "He presented my idea as his own and stole my thunder during the meeting."

The apple of my eye - Someone who is cherished and loved deeply. Example: "My daughter is the apple of my eye. I love her more than anything."

Up in the air - Something that is uncertain or undecided. Example: "The date for the meeting is still up in the air. We haven't finalised it yet."

CHAPTER FOUR

IDIOMS AND PROVERBS

4.2 Animal-Based Idioms

As quiet as a mouse - Very quiet or silent. Example: "She sneaked into the room as quiet as a mouse, hoping not to wake anyone up."

Like a fish out of water - Feeling uncomfortable or out of place in a certain situation. Example: "At the fancy gala, he felt like a fish out of water because he wasn't used to such formal events."

The elephant in the room - An obvious problem or issue that people are avoiding. Example: "Everyone was aware of the budget cuts, but nobody wanted to discuss the elephant in the room."

A bird's-eye view - A panoramic or overall perspective. Example: "From the top of the hill, we had a bird's-eye view of the entire city."

Like a bull in a china shop - Clumsy or careless in one's actions. Example: "He barged into the delicate antique store like a bull in a china shop, knocking over a display."

Busy as a bee - Very busy and active. Example: "She's always busy as a bee, juggling multiple projects at once."

Stubborn as a mule - Extremely stubborn and unwilling to change one's opinion. Example: "No matter how much we tried to convince him, he remained stubborn as a mule."

Like a cat on hot bricks - Anxious or restless. Example: "She couldn't sit still; she was pacing around like a cat on hot bricks."
The lion's share - The largest or greatest portion. Example: "He did the lion's share of the work, taking on most of the responsibilities."

Let the cat out of the bag - To reveal a secret. Example: "She accidentally let the cat out of the bag and told everyone about the surprise party."

To have a bee in one's bonnet - To be obsessed or preoccupied with something. Example: "He has a bee in his bonnet about recycling and is always encouraging others to do it."

Like a lamb to the slaughter - Unaware of the danger or harm that awaits. Example: "He walked into the scam like a lamb to the slaughter, unaware of the consequences."

CHAPTER FOUR
IDIOMS AND PROVERBS

4.2 Animal-Based Idioms

To have a whale of a time - To have a great and enjoyable experience. Example: "We had a whale of a time at the music festival. It was so much fun!"

Strong as an ox - Physically very strong. Example: "He's been working out at the gym for years and is as strong as an ox."

To take the bull by the horns - To confront a problem directly and with determination. Example: "Instead of avoiding the issue, we need to take the bull by the horns and find a solution."

The bee's knees - Something or someone outstanding or excellent. Example: "The new restaurant in town is the bee's knees. The food is amazing!"

To have butterflies in one's stomach - To feel nervous or anxious. Example: "Before going on stage, she had butterflies in her stomach."

A wolf in sheep's clothing - Someone who appears harmless but is actually dangerous or deceptive. Example: "He seemed friendly, but he turned out to be a wolf in sheep's clothing."

To kill two birds with one stone - To accomplish two things with a single action. Example: "By combining grocery shopping with a workout, she killed two birds with one stone."

To have bats in the belfry - To be crazy or eccentric. Example: "Some people think he has bats in the belfry because of his unusual behaviour."

To let sleeping dogs lie - To avoid bringing up old issues that may cause trouble. Example: "We had a disagreement in the past, but it's better to let sleeping dogs lie and move on."

To be a snake in the grass - To be a deceitful or treacherous person. Example: "Watch out for him; he's a snake in the grass who can't be trusted."

To have a memory like an elephant - To have a very good memory. Example: "She remembers everything I've ever told her. She has a memory like an elephant."

To be like water off a duck's back - To be unaffected by criticism or negative comments. Example: "No matter what they say, it's like water off a duck's back to him. He doesn't let it bother him."

CHAPTER FOUR

IDIOMS AND PROVERBS

4.2 Animal-Based Idioms

To be a sitting duck - To be in a vulnerable or defenceless position. Example: "Without any cover, we were like sitting ducks for the enemy's attack."

To be the black sheep of the family - To be the outcast or the one who is different from the rest. Example: "He's always been the black sheep of the family, going against their traditional values."

To have a dog in the fight - To have a personal stake or interest in a situation. Example: "As a shareholder, I have a dog in the fight and want to see the company succeed."

To go to the dogs - To decline or deteriorate in quality or prosperity. Example: "Since the new management took over, the company has gone to the dogs."

To bark up the wrong tree - To accuse or criticise the wrong person. Example: "He accused me of stealing his wallet, but he's barking up the wrong tree. I had nothing to do with it."

To have ants in one's pants - To be restless or unable to sit still. Example: "He had ants in his pants during the long meeting and kept fidgeting."

To be a night owl - To be someone who stays awake and is active late at night. Example: "She's a night owl and prefers working during the late hours of the night."

To be a fisherman's tale - To be an exaggerated or fictional story. Example: "His story about catching a giant fish was nothing more than a fisherman's tale."

To be a snake oil salesman - To be someone who sells fraudulent or ineffective products. Example: "Be careful with that salesman; he's known for being a snake oil salesman."

To be a can of worms - To be a complex or problematic situation. Example: "The issue of employee layoffs is a can of worms that the company needs to address."

To be the cat's whiskers - To be highly admired or regarded. Example: "She thinks she's the cat's whiskers with her new promotion."

To let the cat out of the bag - To reveal a secret. Example: "She accidentally let the cat out of the bag and told everyone about the surprise party."

CHAPTER FOUR

IDIOMS AND PROVERBS

4.2 Animal-Based Idioms

To be a sitting duck - To be in a vulnerable or defenceless position. Example: "Without any cover, we were like sitting ducks for the enemy's attack."

To be the black sheep of the family - To be the outcast or the one who is different from the rest. Example: "He's always been the black sheep of the family, going against their traditional values."

To have a dog in the fight - To have a personal stake or interest in a situation. Example: "As a shareholder, I have a dog in the fight and want to see the company succeed."

To go to the dogs - To decline or deteriorate in quality or prosperity. Example: "Since the new management took over, the company has gone to the dogs."

To bark up the wrong tree - To accuse or criticise the wrong person. Example: "He accused me of stealing his wallet, but he's barking up the wrong tree. I had nothing to do with it."

To have ants in one's pants - To be restless or unable to sit still. Example: "He had ants in his pants during the long meeting and kept fidgeting."

To be a night owl - To be someone who stays awake and is active late at night. Example: "She's a night owl and prefers working during the late hours of the night."

To be a fisherman's tale - To be an exaggerated or fictional story. Example: "His story about catching a giant fish was nothing more than a fisherman's tale."

To be a snake oil salesman - To be someone who sells fraudulent or ineffective products. Example: "Be careful with that salesman; he's known for being a snake oil salesman."

To be a can of worms - To be a complex or problematic situation. Example: "The issue of employee layoffs is a can of worms that the company needs to address."

To be the cat's whiskers - To be highly admired or regarded. Example: "She thinks she's the cat's whiskers with her new promotion."

To let the cat out of the bag - To reveal a secret. Example: "She accidentally let the cat out of the bag and told everyone about the surprise party."

CHAPTER FOUR
IDIOMS AND PROVERBS
4.2 Animal-Based Idioms

To be a lone wolf - To prefer being alone rather than being part of a group. Example: "He's always been a lone wolf, preferring solitude over socialising."

To be as slippery as an eel - To be evasive or difficult to pin down. Example: "He tried to avoid answering the question and was as slippery as an eel."

To be as quiet as a church mouse - To be extremely quiet or silent. Example: "During the meeting, she sat as quiet as a church mouse, not uttering a single word."

To be like a dog with a bone - To be persistent and unwilling to let go of something. Example: "Once he gets an idea in his head, he's like a dog with a bone. He won't give up."

To be as sly as a fox - To be cunning or deceitful. Example: "You can't trust him; he's as sly as a fox and always has an ulterior motive."

To be as busy as a beaver - To be very busy and hardworking. Example: "She's as busy as a beaver, always taking on new projects and responsibilities."

To be the top dog - To be the most important or powerful person in a group. Example: "After years of hard work, he finally became the top dog in the company."

To have the memory of a goldfish - To have a very poor memory. Example: "I have the memory of a goldfish; I can't remember what I had for breakfast."

To have a face like a bulldog chewing a wasp - To have a grumpy or displeased facial expression. Example: "He's always complaining; he has a face like a bulldog chewing a wasp."

To be a bull-headed - To be stubborn or obstinate. Example: "No matter what I say, he refuses to listen. He's bull-headed."

To be as free as a bird - To be completely free and unrestricted. Example: "After retiring, he felt as free as a bird with no responsibilities or commitments."

To be as quiet as the grave - To be completely silent or hushed. Example: "The library was as quiet as the grave; you could hear a pin drop."

To be as slow as a snail - To be very slow in movement or progress. Example: "The construction work is progressing as slow as a snail; it's taking forever."

CHAPTER FOUR

IDIOMS AND PROVERBS

4.3 Weather-Related Idioms

Under the weather - Feeling unwell or sick. Example: "I can't come to the party tonight; I'm feeling a bit under the weather."

Storm in a teacup - A small or insignificant problem that is blown out of proportion. Example: "Don't worry about their argument; it's just a storm in a teacup."

Every cloud has a silver lining - There is something positive in every negative situation. Example: "I lost my job, but every cloud has a silver lining; it gave me the opportunity to pursue a new career."

Come rain or shine - Regardless of any circumstances or weather conditions. Example: "I promised to be there for you, come rain or shine."

On cloud nine - Extremely happy or joyful. Example: "When she received the job offer, she was on cloud nine."

Snowed under - Overwhelmed with a lot of work or tasks. Example: "I won't be able to join you for lunch; I'm snowed under with deadlines."

Weather the storm - To survive a difficult or challenging situation. Example: "It's been a tough year, but we managed to weather the storm and come out stronger."

A ray of sunshine - Someone or something that brings happiness or positivity. Example: "Her cheerful personality is always a ray of sunshine on gloomy days."

Break the ice - To initiate or start a conversation or interaction. Example: "He told a joke to break the ice and make everyone feel more comfortable."

In the eye of the storm - In the midst of a difficult or chaotic situation. Example: "She remained calm and composed in the eye of the storm."

Fair-weather friend - Someone who is only supportive or friendly during good times. Example: "He's not a true friend; he's just a fair-weather friend who disappears when things get tough."

Weather the cold - To endure or tolerate difficult or harsh conditions. Example: "The homeless population must weather the cold winter nights without proper shelter."

CHAPTER FOUR

IDIOMS AND PROVERBS

4.3 Weather-Related Idioms

Head in the clouds - To be daydreaming or not paying attention. Example: "During the lecture, his head was in the clouds, and he didn't hear a word."

On thin ice - In a risky or precarious situation. Example: "He's on thin ice with his boss after missing multiple deadlines."

Like a breath of fresh air - Something or someone that is refreshing or revitalising. Example: "Her positive attitude is like a breath of fresh air in the office."

Face like thunder - To have an angry or displeased facial expression. Example: "When she saw the mess, she had a face like thunder."

Weather the elements - To endure and survive challenging weather conditions. Example: "Mountaineers must be well-prepared to weather the elements during their expeditions."

Keep a stiff upper lip - To remain brave and resolute in difficult times. Example: "Even though he was disappointed, he kept a stiff upper lip and continued with his work."

Bolt from the blue - A sudden and unexpected event. Example: "The news of her promotion was a bolt from the blue; she wasn't expecting it."

Chase rainbows - To pursue unrealistic or impractical goals. Example: "Instead of chasing It's raining cats and dogs - It's raining heavily. Example: "We were planning a picnic, but it started raining cats and dogs, so we had to cancel."

Every cloud has a silver lining - Every difficult or negative situation has a positive aspect. Example: "I lost my job, but every cloud has a silver lining; it gave me the opportunity to pursue a new career."

A storm in a teacup - A situation that is exaggerated or blown out of proportion. Example: "Don't worry about their argument; it's just a storm in a teacup. It will blow over soon."

Break the ice - To initiate or ease tension in a social situation. Example: "To break the ice at the party, I started a conversation about everyone's favourite movies."

On cloud nine - To be extremely happy or joyful. Example: "When she got accepted into her dream university, she was on cloud nine."

CHAPTER FOUR

IDIOMS AND PROVERBS

4.3 Weather-Related Idioms

To weather the storm - To endure and survive a difficult period or situation. Example: "Despite facing financial challenges, the company managed to weather the storm and stay afloat."

As right as rain - Completely fine or in good health. Example: "After a good night's sleep, I felt as right as rain in the morning."

Weather the storm - To successfully overcome a difficult situation or problem. Example: "Despite the setbacks, they managed to weather the storm and complete the project."

In the eye of the storm - In the middle of a chaotic or turbulent situation. Example: "During the negotiations, she remained calm and composed in the eye of the storm."

Fair-weather friend - Someone who is only supportive or friendly during good times. Example: "He's not a reliable friend; he's just a fair-weather friend who disappears when things get tough."

A ray of sunshine - Someone or something that brings happiness or joy. Example: "Her smile is like a ray of sunshine; it brightens up everyone's day."

To be on thin ice - To be in a risky or precarious situation. Example: "He's already late for work; if he arrives late again, he'll be on thin ice with his boss."

Once in a blue moon - Very rarely or infrequently. Example: "I only see my old friends from school once in a blue moon."

Save it for a rainy day - To save something for future use or need. Example: "Instead of spending all your money, save some for a rainy day."

To be snowed under - To be overwhelmed with a large amount of work or tasks. Example: "I can't go out this weekend; I'm snowed under with assignments."

Take a rain check - To postpone or reschedule a plan or invitation. Example: "I'm busy tonight, but can I take a rain check and meet up with you next week?"

Shoot the breeze - To have a casual and relaxed conversation. Example: "Let's sit on the porch and shoot the breeze while enjoying the evening breeze."

CHAPTER FOUR

IDIOMS AND PROVERBS

4.3 Weather-Related Idioms

A baptism of fire - An intense or challenging initiation or introduction to something new. Example: "Her first day at the new job was a baptism of fire with multiple urgent tasks."

It's raining cats and dogs - It's raining heavily. Example: "We were planning a picnic, but it started raining cats and dogs, so we had to cancel."

A storm in a teacup - A situation that is exaggerated or blown out of proportion. Example: "Don't worry about their argument; it's just a storm in a teacup. It will blow over soon."

Break the ice - To initiate or ease tension in a social situation. Example: "To break the ice at the party, I started a conversation about everyone's favourite movies."

On cloud nine - To be extremely happy or joyful. Example: "When she got accepted into her dream university, she was on cloud nine."

To weather the storm - To endure and survive a difficult period or situation. Example: "Despite facing financial challenges, the company managed to weather the storm and stay afloat."

As right as rain - Completely fine or in good health. Example: "After a good night's sleep, I felt as right as rain in the morning."

In the eye of the storm - In the middle of a chaotic or turbulent situation. Example: "During the negotiations, she remained calm and composed in the eye of the storm."

Fair-weather friend - Someone who is only supportive or friendly during good times. Example: "He's not a reliable friend; he's just a fair-weather friend who disappears when things get tough."

A ray of sunshine - Someone or something that brings happiness or joy. Example: "Her smile is like a ray of sunshine; it brightens up everyone's day."

CHAPTER FOUR

IDIOMS AND PROVERBS

4.3 Weather-Related Idioms

To be on thin ice - To be in a risky or precarious situation. Example: "He's already late for work; if he arrives late again, he'll be on thin ice with his boss."

Save it for a rainy day - To save something for future use or need. Example: "Instead of spending all your money, save some for a rainy day."

Take a rain check - To postpone or reschedule a plan or invitation. Example: "I'm busy tonight, but can I take a rain check and meet up with you next week?"

A baptism of fire - An intense or challenging initiation or introduction to something new. Example: "Her first day at the new job was a baptism of fire with multiple urgent tasks."

CHAPTER 2
IDIOMS AND PROVERBS

4.4 Food and Drink Idioms

A piece of cake - Something that is very easy. Example: "Don't worry about the test; it's a piece of cake."

To spill the beans - To reveal a secret or confidential information. Example: "I accidentally spilled the beans about the surprise party."

To be full of beans - To have a lot of energy or enthusiasm. Example: "Despite the long day, he's still full of beans."

To be the apple of someone's eye - To be someone's favourite or most cherished person. Example: "Her granddaughter is the apple of her eye; she adores her."

To go bananas - To become very excited, agitated, or wild. Example: "When her favourite band came on stage, the crowd went bananas."

To bring home the bacon - To earn a living or provide financial support. Example: "He works two jobs to bring home the bacon for his family."

To butter someone up - To flatter or praise someone in order to gain favour. Example: "He's always buttering up the boss to get promotions."

To be in a pickle - To be in a difficult or tricky situation. Example: "I'm in a pickle; I accidentally locked my keys inside the car."

To be as cool as a cucumber - To be calm and composed, especially in stressful situations. Example: "Even in a crisis, she remains as cool as a cucumber."

To be the salt of the earth - To be a genuinely good and honest person. Example: "He's the salt of the earth; he's always there to help others."

To have a sweet tooth - To have a strong craving for sugary foods. Example: "I can't resist desserts; I have a sweet tooth."

To go pear-shaped - To go wrong or become a disaster. Example: "Everything was going well until it all went pear-shaped."

To have egg on your face - To be embarrassed or humiliated by something you did. Example: "I made a mistake in my presentation and ended up with egg on my face."

CHAPTER FOUR

IDIOMS AND PROVERBS

4.4 Food and Drink Idioms

To be like two peas in a pod - To be very similar or nearly identical. Example: "The twins are like two peas in a pod; they even finish each other's sentences."

To spice things up - To make something more exciting or interesting. Example: "Let's spice things up by trying a new restaurant tonight."

To go with the flow - To adapt or accept a situation without resistance. Example: "Instead of worrying, she prefers to go with the flow and see how things unfold."

To be a tough cookie - To be a strong and resilient person. Example: "She went through a lot of challenges, but she's a tough cookie."

To have your cake and eat it too - To want to have or enjoy two conflicting things at the same time. Example: "You can't expect to have your cake and eat it too; you have to make a choice."

To be in hot water - To be in trouble or facing consequences. Example: "He forgot to submit the report; now he's in hot water with his boss."

To be as fresh as a daisy - To be energetic and well-rested. Example: "After a good night's sleep, I woke up as fresh as a daisy."

To be as cool as a cucumber - To be calm and composed, especially in stressful situations. Example: "Even during the exam, she remained as cool as a cucumber."

To be the cream of the crop - To be the best or the highest quality. Example: "Out of all the applicants, she was the cream of the crop."

To have your cake and eat it - To want to have or enjoy two conflicting things at the same time. Example: "He wants to retire early and travel the world, but he also wants to save money; he can't have his cake and eat it too."

To be a tough nut to crack - To be a difficult problem or person to understand or solve. Example: "The puzzle was a tough nut to crack; it took me hours to solve it."

To have bigger fish to fry - To have more important or pressing matters to attend to. Example: "I can't help you right now; I have bigger fish to fry."

CHAPTER FOUR

IDIOMS AND PROVERBS

4.4 Food and Drink Idioms

To be in a stew - To be worried or anxious. Example: "She's been in a stew ever since she lost her wallet."

To have a finger in every pie - To be involved in many different activities or projects. Example: "He's a busy entrepreneur; he has a finger in every pie."

To go against the grain - To do something contrary to the usual or expected way. Example: "She always goes against the grain and challenges traditional ideas."

To be the icing on the cake - To be the extra and enjoyable addition to something that is already good. Example: "Getting a promotion was great, but the salary increase was the icing on the cake."

To have all your eggs in one basket - To have all your resources or hopes invested in a single thing. Example: "He invested all his savings in one company; he put all his eggs in one basket."

To be as flat as a pancake - To be completely flat or deflated. Example: "After being in storage for years, the basketball was as flat as a pancake."

To be like a kid in a candy store - To be extremely excited or delighted. Example: "When she entered the bookstore, she was like a kid in a candy store."

To be as red as a beetroot - To be extremely embarrassed or blushing. Example: "When she tripped in front of everyone, she turned as red as a beetroot."

To go off like a rocket - To become angry or explode with anger suddenly. Example: "When he found out about the broken vase, he went off like a rocket."

To be as sour as vinegar - To be grumpy or bad-tempered. Example: "He woke up on the wrong side of the bed and has been as sour as vinegar all morning."

To take something with a pinch of salt - To be sceptical or not fully believe something. Example: "He tends to exaggerate, so I take his stories with a pinch of salt."

To be the cream of the pudding - To be the best or most outstanding part. Example: "The final chapter of the book is the cream of the pudding; it ties everything together."

CHAPTER 2
IDIOMS AND PROVERBS

4.4 Food and Drink Idioms

To be in a jam - To be in a difficult or problematic situation. Example: "I'm in a jam; I locked myself out of the house."

To have a bun in the oven - To be pregnant. Example: "She's excited to announce that she has a bun in the oven."

To be as dry as a bone - To be completely dry, lacking moisture. Example: "After the long drought, the field was as dry as a bone."

To be like chalk and cheese - To be completely different or opposite. Example: "The twins are like chalk and cheese; they have nothing in common."

To be as flat as a pancake - To be without any noticeable features or excitement. Example: "The party was a flop; it was as flat as a pancake."

To eat humble pie - To admit one's mistake or defeat and apologise. Example: "After realising his error, he had to eat humble pie and apologise."

To have a skeleton in the closet - To have a hidden or embarrassing secret. Example: "No one knew about her past; she had a skeleton in the closet."

To have a lot on your plate - To have a lot of tasks or responsibilities to deal with. Example: "She's juggling work, family, and studies; she has a lot on her plate."

To be like marmite - To either be loved or hated, with no in-between. Example: "His comedy style is like marmite; people either find it hilarious or can't stand it."

To be the cherry on top - To be the extra and delightful addition to something already good. Example: "Winning the lottery would be the cherry on top of an already amazing year."

To be as hot as mustard - To be enthusiastic or energetic. Example: "She's always ready to help; she's as hot as mustard."

To wine and dine - To entertain someone lavishly, especially by providing them with food and drinks. Example: "He wanted to impress his clients, so he took them out to wine and dine."

CHAPTER FOUR
IDIOMS AND PROVERBS

4.5 Proverbs and Sayings

A penny saved is a penny earned. - Saving money is as valuable as earning it. Example: Instead of buying expensive gadgets, she saves her money for future investments.

Don't count your chickens before they hatch - Don't assume something will happen before it actually does. Example: He was already planning his victory speech before the election results were announced. Don't count your chickens before they hatch!

Every cloud has a silver lining - Even in difficult times, there is usually something positive to be found. Example: Despite losing her job, she discovered a new career opportunity. Every cloud has a silver lining.

Actions speak louder than words - What someone does is more important than what they say. Example: He promised to help, but his actions speak louder than words as he never showed up.

All's fair in love and war - In certain situations, anything is acceptable, even if it might seem unfair. Example: She used every trick in the book to win the argument. All's fair in love and war.

When in Rome, do as the Romans do - Adapt to the customs and behaviour of the place you're in. Example: Even though she found it strange, she decided to eat with her hands since it was the local custom. When in Rome, do as the Romans do.

Don't put all your eggs in one basket - Don't rely on a single thing or plan; have alternatives. Example: Instead of investing all his money in one business, he diversified his investments. Don't put all your eggs in one basket.

The early bird catches the worm - Being proactive and starting early gives you an advantage. Example: She always arrives at work before everyone else to get a head start. The early bird catches the worm.

It's no use crying over spilled milk - There's no point in being upset over something that has already happened and cannot be changed. Example: He lost the game, but it's no use crying over spilled milk. He'll do better next time.

A stitch in time saves nine - Taking care of a problem early prevents it from becoming worse. Example: He repaired the leaky faucet immediately, saving himself from a bigger plumbing issue. A stitch in time saves nine.

CHAPTER FOUR

IDIOMS AND PROVERBS

4.5 Proverbs and Sayings

Beauty is in the eye of the beholder - Different people have different opinions on what is beautiful. Example: She didn't like the painting, but her friend thought it was stunning. Beauty is in the eye of the beholder.

Better late than never - It's better to do something late than to not do it at all. Example: He finally apologised for his mistake, even though it took him months. Better late than never.

Curiosity killed the cat - Being too curious or nosy can lead to trouble. Example: She couldn't resist opening the mysterious package, and it turned out to be a prank. Curiosity killed the cat.

Don't bite the hand that feeds you - Don't harm or offend someone who helps or supports you. Example: He insulted his boss, forgetting that he was the one who recommended him for the promotion. Don't bite the hand that feeds you.

Don't judge a book by its cover - Don't form an opinion based solely on appearance. Example: The old house may look rundown, but inside it's beautifully renovated. Don't judge a book by its cover.

Every dog has its day - Everyone will have their moment of success or triumph. Example: He had faced many failures, but eventually, his hard work paid off. Every dog has its day.

Haste makes waste - Rushing can lead to mistakes or inefficiency. Example: She hurriedly packed her bag and forgot to bring her passport. Haste makes waste.

Look before you leap - Think carefully before taking action. Example: He wanted to invest all his savings in a new business, but his friend advised him to look before he leaped.

Make hay while the sun shines - Take advantage of an opportunity while it lasts. Example: The weather was perfect for a picnic, so they made hay while the sun shone and enjoyed the day.

Out of sight, out of mind - People tend to forget about things or people that are not visible. Example: She moved to another city, and her old friends slowly forgot about her. Out of sight, out of mind.

CHAPTER FOUR

IDIOMS AND PROVERBS

4.5 Proverbs and Sayings

Practice makes perfect - Repeating something helps improve your skills. Example: She practiced playing the piano every day and eventually became a skilled musician. Practice makes perfect.

Rome wasn't built in a day - Big achievements take time and effort. Example: Learning a new language requires patience and consistency. Rome wasn't built in a day.

The early bird gets the worm - Those who take action early have an advantage. Example: She arrived at the store early and got the best deals during the sale. The early bird gets the worm.

There's no smoke without fire - There is usually some truth to rumours or allegations. Example: The media reported on corruption allegations, and they say there's no smoke without fire.

When the going gets tough, the tough get going - In difficult situations, resilient people become even more determined. Example: Despite facing numerous setbacks, he never gave up and kept working harder. When the going gets tough, the tough get going.

You can't have your cake and eat it too - You can't enjoy or possess two conflicting things at the same time. Example: She wanted to go on vacation and save money, but she realised she can't have her cake and eat it too.

You reap what you sow - Your actions have consequences. Example: If you work hard and study diligently, you'll reap what you sow and achieve good results.

A leopard can't change its spots - People's inherent nature or character traits do not change easily. Example: He promised to be more organised, but he couldn't help his messy habits. A leopard can't change its spots.

A watched pot never boils - Time feels slower when you're eagerly waiting for something. Example: He kept checking his email for a response, but a watched pot never boils. Patience is needed.

You can't make an omelette without breaking eggs - In order to achieve something, sacrifices or compromises are necessary. Example: The business required significant investments, and they knew they couldn't make an omelette without breaking eggs.

CHAPTER FOUR

IDIOMS AND PROVERBS

4.5 Proverbs and Sayings

An apple a day keeps the doctor away - Eating healthily can help prevent illness. Example: She makes sure to eat fruits and vegetables every day. An apple a day keeps the doctor away.

As fit as a fiddle - In excellent physical condition. Example: He exercises regularly and eats well, so he's as fit as a fiddle.

Barking dogs seldom bite - Those who make the most noise are often the least harmful. Example: He threatened to sue, but he didn't take any further action. Barking dogs seldom bite.

Don't rock the boat - Avoid causing trouble or disrupting a stable situation. Example: They were having a peaceful discussion until he brought up a controversial topic. Don't rock the boat.

Easier said than done - Something may sound simple in theory but is challenging in practice. Example: He advised her to confront her fears, but she knew it was easier said than done.

Every little helps - Even small contributions or efforts can make a difference. Example: She donated a small amount to the charity, knowing that every little helps.

Fortune favours the brave - Taking risks often leads to success or good fortune. Example: She decided to start her own business, believing that fortune favours the brave.

Give credit where credit is due - Acknowledge and appreciate someone's efforts or achievements. Example: He praised his colleague for the excellent presentation, giving credit where credit was due.

If the cap fits, wear it - If something said applies to you, accept it. Example: She criticised his laziness, and he felt guilty because if the cap fits, wear it.

It takes two to tango - Cooperation or participation from both parties is necessary. Example: They argued about who was responsible for the conflict, but it takes two to tango.

CHAPTER FOUR

IDIOMS AND PROVERBS

4.5 Proverbs and Sayings

Keep your friends close and your enemies closer - Be vigilant and aware of those who might wish you harm. Example: He maintained a cordial relationship with his rival to stay informed. Keep your friends close and your enemies closer.

Laughter is the best medicine - Humour and laughter can improve one's mood and well-being. Example: They watched a comedy show to cheer themselves up since laughter is the best medicine.

Let sleeping dogs lie - Avoid stirring up old conflicts or problems. Example: They decided not to bring up past arguments and let sleeping dogs lie.

No man is an island - Humans need social interaction and community. Example: He realised he couldn't accomplish everything alone since no man is an island.

Patience is a virtue - Being patient is considered a positive quality. Example: He waited calmly in the long queue, knowing that patience is a virtue.

The grass is always greener on the other side - People tend to believe that others have a better situation than their own. Example: She envied her friend's job, but she didn't realise the grass is always greener on the other side.

There's no time like the present -The present moment is the best time to take action. Example: He decided to start working on his dream project, realising there's no time like the present.

Too many cooks spoil the broth -Too many people involved in a task can lead to confusion and inefficiency. Example: They had conflicting ideas and couldn't agree on the final design. Too many cooks spoil the broth.

What goes around comes around - The consequences of one's actions will eventually return to them. Example: He spread rumours about his colleague, and later he faced similar gossip. What goes around comes around.

Where there's smoke, there's fire - If there are signs or indications of a problem, it is likely to be true. Example: They heard rumours about budget cuts, and where there's smoke, there's fire.

CHAPTER FOUR

IDIOMS AND PROVERBS

4.5 Proverbs and Sayings

Keep your friends close and your enemies closer - Be vigilant and aware of those who might wish you harm. Example: He maintained a cordial relationship with his rival to stay informed. Keep your friends close and your enemies closer.

Laughter is the best medicine - Humour and laughter can improve one's mood and well-being. Example: They watched a comedy show to cheer themselves up since laughter is the best medicine.

Let sleeping dogs lie - Avoid stirring up old conflicts or problems. Example: They decided not to bring up past arguments and let sleeping dogs lie.

No man is an island - Humans need social interaction and community. Example: He realised he couldn't accomplish everything alone since no man is an island.

Patience is a virtue - Being patient is considered a positive quality. Example: He waited calmly in the long queue, knowing that patience is a virtue.

The grass is always greener on the other side - People tend to believe that others have a better situation than their own. Example: She envied her friend's job, but she didn't realise the grass is always greener on the other side.

There's no time like the present - The present moment is the best time to take action. Example: He decided to start working on his dream project, realising there's no time like the present.

Too many cooks spoil the broth - Too many people involved in a task can lead to confusion and inefficiency. Example: They had conflicting ideas and couldn't agree on the final design. Too many cooks spoil the broth.

What goes around comes around - The consequences of one's actions will eventually return to them. Example: He spread rumours about his colleague, and later he faced similar gossip. What goes around comes around.

Where there's smoke, there's fire - If there are signs or indications of a problem, it is likely to be true. Example: They heard rumours about budget cuts, and where there's smoke, there's fire.

CHAPTER V

LEARNING AND MASTERING BRITISH ENGLISH

CHAPTER FIVE

LEARNING AND MASTERING UK ENGLISH

5.1 Immersion and Exposure to UK Culture

One of the best ways to learn advanced English is to immerse yourself in the culture and language. Here are some ideas to help you to know where to start.

Watch British TV shows and films: Explore popular British TV series, documentaries, and films to familiarise yourself with British accents, slang, and cultural references.
Watch shows like "Downton Abbey," "Sherlock," or films like "The King's Speech" to immerse yourself in British storytelling and culture.

Listen to British music and podcasts: Tune in to British radio stations, podcasts, and music to expose yourself to the language and accents while enjoying British artists and conversations.
Listen to music from British bands like The Beatles, Adele, or podcasts like "No Such Thing as a Fish" to engage with British culture and language.

Read British literature: Dive into classic and contemporary British literature, including novels, plays, and poetry, to gain insights into British culture, history, and literary traditions.
Read works by British authors like William Shakespeare, Jane Austen, or contemporary writers like J.K. Rowling.

Follow British news outlets: Stay updated on current events in the UK by reading news articles from reputable British news outlets, such as BBC News, The Guardian, or The Times.
Browse the BBC News website or download the BBC News app to access British news articles and reports.

Engage in social media communities: Join online communities, forums, and social media groups dedicated to UK culture and language learning to connect with native speakers and gain cultural insights.
Participate in Facebook groups like "UK Culture Enthusiasts" or follow Instagram accounts that showcase British landmarks and traditions.

Visit British museums and exhibitions: Explore museums and exhibitions that showcase British history, art, and culture to gain firsthand knowledge and experiences.
Visit the British Museum in London or the National Museum of Scotland in Edinburgh to discover artifacts and artworks that depict British heritage.

CHAPTER FIVE

LEARNING AND MASTERING UK ENGLISH

5.1 Immersion and Exposure to UK Culture

Travel to the UK: Plan a trip to the UK to immerse yourself in the language, culture, and daily life of the country. Explore cities, interact with locals, and visit landmarks.
Visit iconic sites like Buckingham Palace, Stonehenge, or the Tower of London while exploring different regions of the UK.

Engage in British cuisine: Try British dishes and beverages to experience the flavours and traditions of British cuisine.
Enjoy a traditional English breakfast, sample fish and chips, or try a cup of English tea with scones and clotted cream.

Follow British influencers and vloggers: Subscribe to YouTube channels and social media accounts of British influencers and vloggers who share insights into British culture, lifestyle, and language.
Follow vloggers like "The Michalaks" or lifestyle influencers like Soella to see glimpses of British daily life and learn colloquial English expressions.

Learn about British history and landmarks: Familiarise yourself with the history of the UK and iconic landmarks to understand their cultural significance and enhance your language learning.
Study the history of British monarchy, learn about Stonehenge, or explore the significance of the Tower Bridge.

Engage in language exchange programs: Participate in language exchange programs that connect you with native English speakers from the UK. Interact with them to improve your language skills and gain cultural insights.
Join language exchange platforms like Tandem or HelloTalk to find language partners from the UK for conversation practice.

Volunteer in British communities: Find volunteer opportunities in British communities or cultural organisations to engage with locals, contribute to community projects, and immerse yourself in the local culture.
EVolunteer at a local charity, community centre, or cultural festival to connect with British individuals and gain cultural experiences.

CHAPTER FIVE
LEARNING AND MASTERING UK ENGLISH

5.1 Immersion and Exposure to UK Culture

Follow British comedy and humour: Explore British comedy shows, stand-up performances, and humorous literature to appreciate British wit and comedy traditions.
Watch comedy panel shows like "QI" or stand-up performances by British comedians like Eddie Izzard or Ricky Gervais.

Engage in British sports and traditions: Learn about popular British sports like football, cricket, or rugby, and familiarise yourself with British traditions like afternoon tea or the Highland Games.
Attend a football match, watch a cricket game, or experience the tradition of afternoon tea in a British tearoom.

Learn about British etiquette: Study British etiquette and social norms to understand cultural nuances and behaviours in different social settings.
Learn about British greetings, table manners, and appropriate behaviour in formal and informal settings.

Connect with British pen pals: Find pen pals from the UK to exchange letters or emails and have conversations about each other's cultures, traditions, and daily life.
Join online pen pal platforms or language exchange forums to connect with British individuals interested in cultural exchange.

Participate in language immersion programs: Enrol in language immersion programs that offer immersive experiences in the UK, allowing you to learn English while living with a British host family or attending language classes.
Example: Participate in a summer language immersion program in London, where you can attend language classes, engage in cultural activities, and interact with locals.

Explore British-themed exhibitions or events abroad: Look for British-themed exhibitions, cultural festivals, or events taking place outside of the UK to experience British culture and traditions in your own location.
Attend a British film festival, visit a British-themed exhibition at a local museum, or participate in a British cuisine festival.

Immerse yourself in British media: Surround yourself with British media, including books, magazines, newspapers, music, and films, to create an immersive environment that exposes you to the language and culture.
Set your preferred language on your devices to English, read British magazines or newspapers, and create playlists of British music.

CHAPTER FIVE
LEARNING AND MASTERING UK ENGLISH

5.1 Immersion and Exposure to UK Culture

Follow British comedy and humour: Explore British comedy shows, stand-up performances, and humorous literature to appreciate British wit and comedy traditions.
Watch comedy panel shows like "QI" or stand-up performances by British comedians like Eddie Izzard or Ricky Gervais.

Engage in British sports and traditions: Learn about popular British sports like football, cricket, or rugby, and familiarise yourself with British traditions like afternoon tea or the Highland Games.
Attend a football match, watch a cricket game, or experience the tradition of afternoon tea in a British tearoom.

Learn about British etiquette: Study British etiquette and social norms to understand cultural nuances and behaviours in different social settings.
Learn about British greetings, table manners, and appropriate behaviour in formal and informal settings.

Connect with British pen pals: Find pen pals from the UK to exchange letters or emails and have conversations about each other's cultures, traditions, and daily life.
Join online pen pal platforms or language exchange forums to connect with British individuals interested in cultural exchange.

Participate in language immersion programs: Enrol in language immersion programs that offer immersive experiences in the UK, allowing you to learn English while living with a British host family or attending language classes.
Participate in a summer language immersion program in London, where you can attend language classes, engage in cultural activities, and interact with locals.

Explore British-themed exhibitions or events abroad: Look for British-themed exhibitions, cultural festivals, or events taking place outside of the UK to experience British culture and traditions in your own location.
Attend a British film festival, visit a British-themed exhibition at a local museum, or participate in a British cuisine festival.

Immerse yourself in British media: Surround yourself with British media, including books, magazines, newspapers, music, and films, to create an immersive environment that exposes you to the language and culture.
Set your preferred language on your devices to English, read British magazines or newspapers, and create playlists of British music.

CHAPTER FIVE

LEARNING AND MASTERING UK ENGLISH

5.2 Conversations and Language Exchanges

Practice Speaking: Find opportunities to speak English with native speakers or language exchange partners. Join conversation groups, attend language meetups, or even practice speaking with yourself. The more you practice speaking, the more confident you'll become.

Effective ways to practice speaking and improve your English language skills, along with examples and explanations:

Engage in conversations with native speakers: Seek opportunities to interact with native English speakers to practice speaking in a natural and authentic way.
Join conversation groups or language exchange programs to have conversations with native speakers.

Practice speaking with a language partner: Find a language partner who is also learning English and engage in regular conversation practice.
Meet with your language partner once a week to have conversations on various topics.

Participate in language exchanges: Join language exchange events or platforms where you can meet native English speakers who are learning your native language. Take turns practicing each other's languages.
Attend a language exchange meetup and spend half of the time speaking in English and the other half speaking in your partner's language.

Take a speaking-focused English course: Enrol in a course or program that specifically focuses on improving speaking skills through structured lessons and speaking activities.
Join an intensive English speaking course that includes role-playing, discussions, and presentations.

Record and listen to yourself: Use a recording device or app to record your voice while speaking in English. Listen to the recordings to identify areas for improvement.
Record yourself giving a short presentation in English and analyse your pronunciation and fluency.

CHAPTER FIVE

LEARNING AND MASTERING UK ENGLISH

5.2 Conversations and Language Exchanges

Practice speaking in front of a mirror: Stand in front of a mirror and practice speaking in English, focusing on your pronunciation, facial expressions, and body language.
Practice giving a speech or presentation in front of a mirror to improve your confidence and delivery.

Utilise language learning apps: Use mobile apps that provide speaking exercises and opportunities for conversation practice with virtual tutors or language bots.
Use language learning apps like Duolingo, HelloTalk, or Babbel to practice speaking English with interactive lessons and chatbots.

Join speaking clubs or Toastmasters: Join local speaking clubs or Toastmasters International to improve your public speaking skills and gain confidence in expressing yourself in English.
Attend a Toastmasters meeting and participate in impromptu speaking sessions or prepared speeches.

Role-play different scenarios: Practice role-playing various scenarios in English, such as ordering food in a restaurant, making a phone call, or negotiating a business deal.
Pair up with a friend and take turns playing different roles to practice common English conversations.

Use language learning websites: Access online platforms that offer speaking exercises, conversation prompts, and pronunciation drills.
Visit websites like FluentU, ESL Speaking, or BBC Learning English to find speaking activities and resources.

Watch and mimic native speakers: Watch movies, TV shows, or online videos featuring native English speakers, and try to imitate their pronunciation, intonation, and speaking style.
Watch a British TV series and practice speaking like the characters, mimicking their accents and expressions.

Practice speaking in everyday situations: Use English in your daily life, such as ordering coffee at a café, asking for directions, or engaging in small talk with colleagues.
Strike up conversations with English speakers you encounter in your daily routines, such as in shops or on public transportation.

CHAPTER FIVE

LEARNING AND MASTERING UK ENGLISH

5.2 Conversations and Language Exchanges

Join online discussion forums: Participate in online forums or social media groups related to your interests, and actively engage in discussions in English. Join an English language learners' forum or a group discussing topics you're passionate about, and contribute to the conversations.

Attend language immersion programs or camps: Join language immersion programs where you are surrounded by English speakers and practice speaking in real-life situations. Enrol in an English language immersion camp or a study abroad program to immerse yourself in an English-speaking environment.

Practice speaking through language games: Play interactive language games that require speaking and conversation, such as word association or storytelling games. Play the "Story Chain" game with friends, where each person adds a sentence to create a story.

Use conversation starters: Prepare a list of conversation starters or topics of interest to initiate discussions with others. Use conversation starters like "What is your favourite book/movie?" or "Tell me about your travel experiences."

Speak with a tutor or language coach: Hire a tutor or language coach who can provide personalised guidance and help improve your speaking skills. Schedule regular sessions with a qualified English tutor who can assess your speaking abilities and provide targeted feedback.

Practice pronunciation and intonation: Focus on improving your pronunciation and intonation by listening to native speakers, practicing phonetic exercises, and using pronunciation apps or resources. Use online resources like Forvo or Pronunciation Studio to practice specific sounds and improve your pronunciation.

CHAPTER FIVE

LEARNING AND MASTERING UK ENGLISH

5.2 Conversations and Language Exchanges

Attend speaking workshops or seminars: Attend workshops or seminars that focus on developing speaking skills and provide opportunities for practical exercises and feedback. Participate in a workshop on public speaking or conversational English to refine your speaking abilities.

Be confident and practice regularly: Build your confidence by speaking English as often as possible and embracing opportunities to practice speaking in different contexts. Remind yourself that making mistakes is a normal part of the learning process and focus on consistent practice to improve your speaking skills over time.

CHAPTER FIVE

LEARNING AND MASTERING UK ENGLISH

5.3 Reading British Literature and Newspapers

1. Follow British newspapers: Read reputable British newspapers to stay updated on current affairs while enhancing your English reading skills. Visit the websites of newspapers like The Guardian, The Times, or BBC News and read articles on topics that interest you.
2. Discuss articles with native speakers: Engage in conversations with native English speakers to practice discussing news articles and literature, exchanging opinions and ideas. Join online forums or language exchange platforms to interact with native speakers and discuss articles you've read.
3. Analyse cultural references: Pay attention to cultural references in British literature and newspapers to better understand British customs, traditions, and historical events. Research references to the "Blitz" in World War II mentioned in a novel and gain a deeper understanding of its significance.
4. Keep a reading journal: Record your thoughts, reflections, and summaries of what you've read to enhance comprehension and track your progress. Write a brief summary of each chapter or article you read, noting down your favourite quotes or memorable passages.
5. Challenge yourself with complex texts: Occasionally tackle more challenging British literary works to push your language skills further and expand your vocabulary. Take on renowned British authors like William Shakespeare or Charles Dickens to delve into their timeless works.
6. Utilise online resources: Access online resources such as e-books, audiobooks, and language learning websites to supplement your reading materials and provide additional support. Use online platforms like Project Gutenberg or Librivox to access free British literature in digital formats.
7. Practice comprehension exercises: Complete comprehension exercises or quizzes related to the literature or articles you've read to reinforce your understanding and test your knowledge. Solve comprehension questions based on a British newspaper article to ensure you've grasped the main ideas and details.
8. Read regularly: Make reading a daily habit to improve your language skills and expand your vocabulary. Set aside 30 minutes every day to read a British novel or newspaper article.
9. Start with easier texts: Begin with simpler literature or news articles and gradually progress to more complex ones as your language proficiency improves. Begin by reading short stories or news summaries before tackling longer novels or in-depth articles.

CHAPTER FIVE

LEARNING AND MASTERING UK ENGLISH

5.3 Reading British Literature and Newspapers part 2

10. Use a dictionary: Keep a dictionary handy to look up unfamiliar words and phrases for better comprehension. When you encounter an unfamiliar word like "perplexed," consult the dictionary to understand its meaning.

11. Take notes: Jot down new vocabulary, idioms, or phrases you come across while reading, and review them later for better retention. Write down the phrase "barking up the wrong tree" and its meaning as you encounter it in a British novel.

12. Analyse sentence structure: Pay attention to sentence construction, grammar usage, and sentence variety to improve your own writing and language fluency. Analyse how complex sentences are used in British literature to express ideas more effectively.

13. Read aloud: Practice reading aloud to improve pronunciation, fluency, and intonation. Read a passage from a British novel out loud, focusing on clear enunciation and proper stress.

14. Join a book club: Engage in discussions with fellow readers to gain insights and different perspectives on British literature. Participate in a book club focused on reading and discussing classic British novels like Jane Austen's "Pride and Prejudice."

15. Explore different genres: Read a variety of genres, including fiction, non-fiction, poetry, and newspapers, to expose yourself to different writing styles and topics. Alternate between reading a historical novel, a collection of British poetry, and a newspaper article on current events.

CHAPTER FIVE

LEARNING AND MASTERING UK ENGLISH

5.4 Watching British Films and TV Shows

Ways to watch British films and TV shows to learn English:

Start with popular British classics: Begin by watching well-known British classics to familiarise yourself with iconic films that have influenced British cinema. Watch films like "Lawrence of Arabia" or "The Third Man" to appreciate classic British filmmaking and storytelling.

Explore British TV dramas: Dive into British TV dramas known for their compelling storytelling, character development, and cultural insights.
Watch acclaimed series like "Sherlock," "Downton Abbey," or "Peaky Blinders" to immerse yourself in British narratives and dialogue.

Watch British comedy shows: Explore British comedy series known for their wit, humour, and unique comedic style.
Enjoy shows like "Fawlty Towers," "Monty Python's Flying Circus," or "The Office" (UK version) to experience British humour and comedic timing.

Discover British period dramas: Explore British period dramas set in different eras to gain insights into British history, customs, and language usage.
Watch series like "Pride and Prejudice," "Victoria," or "The Crown" to immerse yourself in the historical context of British society.

Follow British crime and detective shows: Engage with British crime and detective series, known for their intriguing storylines and complex characters.
Watch shows like "Broadchurch," "Luther," or "Line of Duty" to experience British crime dramas and police procedurals.

Embrace regional accents: Seek out films and TV shows set in different regions of the UK to expose yourself to various British accents and dialects.
Watch "Trainspotting" to hear Scottish accents or "The Full Monty" to experience accents from the North of England.

CHAPTER FIVE

LEARNING AND MASTERING UK ENGLISH

5.4 Watching British Films and TV Shows

Use subtitles strategically: Start by watching with English subtitles to aid comprehension, and gradually reduce reliance on subtitles as your listening skills improve.
Watch with English subtitles and try to identify words and phrases without relying solely on the subtitles.

Engage in post-viewing discussions: Reflect on the films or TV shows you watch and discuss them with friends or language partners to share perspectives and deepen your understanding.
Join a film club or organise a viewing party with friends to discuss themes, characters, and cultural references.

Take notes while watching: Make a habit of jotting down new vocabulary, expressions, and cultural references while watching British films and TV shows.
Keep a notebook or use a note-taking app to record interesting words, phrases, and cultural insights for later review.

Repeat and mimic dialogues: Watch scenes or dialogues multiple times and try to mimic the pronunciation, intonation, and rhythm of the actors' speech.
Select a scene from a film or TV show and repeat the lines out loud, paying attention to the actors' delivery.

Analyse character interactions: Observe the dynamics between characters, their non-verbal cues, and the subtleties of British social interactions.
Analyse the interactions between Sherlock Holmes and Dr. John Watson in "Sherlock" to understand British communication styles.

Engage with British documentaries: Watch British documentaries that explore various subjects, from history and nature to culture and current affairs.
Watch documentaries like "Planet Earth," "Blue Planet," or "The Story of the Jews" to learn about diverse topics while improving your listening skills.

Create a watchlist of British films and shows: Curate a list of British films and TV shows you want to watch, and gradually work your way through the list.
Use platforms like IMDb or Letterboxd to create a watchlist of British films and shows that catch your interest.

CHAPTER FIVE
LEARNING AND MASTERING UK ENGLISH
5.4 Watching British Films and TV Shows

Participate in online forums and communities: Join online forums or communities where you can discuss British films and TV shows, exchange recommendations, and engage with fellow language learners.
Participate in Reddit communities like r/UKTVLAND or dedicated language learning forums to discuss British media and discover new recommendations.

Watch interviews and behind-the-scenes content: Explore interviews, behind-the-scenes footage, and director commentaries related to British films and TV shows to gain insights into the creative process and cultural context.
Watch interviews with British actors or directors discussing their work or explore behind-the-scenes documentaries of popular British productions.

Compare British adaptations: If a British film or TV show is an adaptation of a non-British original, consider watching both versions to compare cultural nuances and language differences.
Watch both the British and American versions of "The Office" to compare the cultural context and humour.

Incorporate variety: Explore a range of genres and styles within British cinema and TV to broaden your exposure to different narratives and language usage.
Watch a British romantic comedy like "Love Actually," a British thriller like "Lock, Stock and Two Smoking Barrels," and a British coming-of-age film like "Billy Elliot."

Use online streaming platforms: Take advantage of online streaming platforms that offer a wide selection of British films and TV shows, including British broadcasters' streaming services.
Access platforms like Netflix, Amason Prime Video, or BBC iPlayer to discover and stream British content.

Watch with English subtitles in challenging scenes: When encountering challenging scenes with fast dialogue or strong accents, use English subtitles to aid comprehension.
Enable English subtitles when watching a film or show with a heavy Scottish accent, such as "Trainspotting."

Enjoy British cinema as entertainment: Ultimately, remember to enjoy the process of watching British films and TV shows, appreciating them as forms of entertainment while learning the language and culture.
Relax, grab some popcorn, and immerse yourself in the captivating world of British storytelling.

CHAPTER FIVE

LEARNING AND MASTERING UK ENGLISH

5.5 Online Resources and Language Learning Apps

Select popular and highly-rated language learning apps that offer comprehensive English courses and interactive exercises. Use apps like Duolingo, Babbel, or Rosetta Stone to practice vocabulary, grammar, and listening skills.

Enrol in online language courses specifically designed to teach English, either through paid platforms or free resources. Take advantage of platforms like Coursera, Udemy, or the British Council's LearnEnglish website, which offer structured English courses.

Join language exchange platforms where you can connect with native English speakers who are learning your native language, and engage in conversations to improve your speaking skills. Platforms like Tandem, HelloTalk, or ConversationExchange facilitate language exchange partnerships.

Listen to English podcasts covering a wide range of topics to improve your listening comprehension and vocabulary. Explore podcasts like "The English We Speak" by the BBC or "Learn English with Podcasts" by EnglishClass101.

Subscribe to YouTube channels that provide English language lessons, pronunciation practice, and cultural insights. Channels like Learn English with Emma or BBC Learning English offer engaging lessons and tutorials.

Join online forums and communities dedicated to English language learning, where you can ask questions, share experiences, and receive support from fellow learners and native speakers. Participate in communities like Reddit's r/EnglishLearning or language learning forums like Fluent in 3 Months.

Utilise online dictionaries, such as Merriam-Webster or Oxford English Dictionary, for quick definitions, word usage, and pronunciation guidance. Look up unfamiliar words or phrases while reading or listening to English content to expand your vocabulary.

Explore websites specifically designed for language learners, offering a variety of exercises, quisses, and interactive activities. Websites like British Council's LearnEnglish or ESL Games provide interactive language learning resources.

CHAPTER FIVE

LEARNING AND MASTERING UK ENGLISH

5.5 Online Resources and Language Learning Apps

Listen to podcasts specifically designed for English language learners, which provide explanations, exercises, and practice opportunities. "EnglishClass101" or "All Ears English" are popular podcasts that offer lessons and conversations for language learners.

Consume authentic English materials such as news articles, blogs, or literature to enhance your reading comprehension and vocabulary. Read articles from reputable news sources like The Guardian or BBC News, or explore blogs in your areas of interest.

Use online language level tests to assess your proficiency and identify areas for improvement. Platforms like Cambridge English Online or EF SET provide free English language level tests.

Utilise apps that focus on vocabulary acquisition, offering word games, flashcards, and vocabulary challenges. Apps like Memrise, Quislet, or Vocabulary.com help expand your vocabulary through interactive exercises.

Use online platforms or language learning apps that provide writing prompts, correction services, and opportunities for feedback. Platforms like Lang-8 or Tandem offer writing practice and allow native speakers to review and provide feedback on your writing.

Attend virtual language exchange events or conversation groups, where you can practice English speaking with native speakers and fellow learners. Platforms like Meetup or Conversation Exchange offer virtual language exchange events and conversation practice opportunities.

Access online platforms that provide video tutorials and lessons on various aspects of English language learning, such as grammar, pronunciation, or idiomatic expressions. Websites like EnglishClass101 or BBC Learning English provide video lessons and tutorials.

Participate in online book clubs focused on English literature, where you can read and discuss English books with fellow language learners. Join online book clubs on platforms like Goodreads or dedicated language learning forums.

CHAPTER FIVE

LEARNING AND MASTERING UK ENGLISH

5.5 Online Resources and Language Learning Apps

Utilise apps specifically designed for pronunciation practice, which offer speech recognition technology and feedback. Apps like ELSA Speak, Speechling, or Sounds: The Pronunciation App provide pronunciation exercises and feedback.

Follow English language learning accounts and native English speakers on social media platforms to expose yourself to authentic language usage and cultural insights. Follow accounts like FluentU, EnglishCentral, or English Today to receive language tips, vocabulary, and cultural content.

Improve your listening skills and enjoy English literature by listening to audiobooks narrated by native English speakers. Use platforms like Audible or Librivox to access a wide range of English audiobooks.

Use apps that provide interactive grammar exercises and explanations to strengthen your grammatical skills. Apps like Grammarly, English Grammar in Use, or Duolingo offer grammar-focused exercises and explanations.

Explore blogs dedicated to English language learning, where you can find tips, resources, and practice exercises. Blogs like FluentU, Espresso English, or English Harmony provide valuable language learning insights and resources.

Join online language challenges, such as vocabulary challenges or writing prompts, to motivate yourself and track your progress. Platforms like Vocabulary.com or language learning communities often organise challenges to encourage language learning engagement.

Access the vast collection of TED Talks and watch presentations given by native English speakers on various subjects to enhance your listening comprehension and learn from inspiring speakers. Explore TED.com and search for talks on topics that interest you.

Utilise online quizzes and interactive language games to make learning English more engaging and enjoyable. Websites like EnglishClub or Fun English Games provide quizzes, word games, and interactive activities.

Use online language learning platforms or apps that allow you to set goals, track your progress, and receive personalised recommendations. Apps like Duolingo, Babbel, or Memrise offer progress tracking features and personalised learning paths.

CHAPTER VI

PRACTICING BRITISH ENGLISH - MOCK CONVERSATIONS

PRACTICING UK ENGLISH

6.1 Role-Playing and Mock Conversations

Discussing a Movie

Talking about a movie you recently watched.

Person A: Have you seen the new superhero movie yet?
Person B: Yes, I watched it last week. The special effects were incredible.
Person A: Did you like the storyline?
Person B: It was decent, but I felt the ending was a bit rushed.

Talking about Family

Sharing information about your family members.

Person A: Do you have any siblings?
Person B: Yes, I have an older brother and a younger sister.
Person A: Are you close to them?
Person B: Yes, we're a tight-knit family. We spend a lot of time together.

Giving and Receiving Directions in a City

Practice giving and following directions in a city.

Person A: Excuse me, how do I get to the nearest museum from here?
Person B: Go straight down this road, then turn right at the traffic lights. It'll be on your left.
Person A: Thank you. Is it within walking distance?
Person B: Yes, it's just a ten-minute walk from here.

Talking about Work

Discussing your profession and workplace.

Person A: What do you do for a living?
Person B: I work as a software engineer for a tech company.
Person A: That sounds interesting. Do you enjoy your job?
Person B: Yes, I love working with technology and solving complex problems.

Planning a Party

Organising a social event and discussing details.

Person A: We should throw a surprise party for Sarah's birthday.
Person B: That's a great idea. Where should we have it?
Person A: How about renting a community centre? It'll give us enough space.

Talking about Technology

Discussing the latest advancements in technology.

Person A: Have you heard about the new smartphone that was released?
Person B: Yes, it has some impressive features, like a high-resolution camera and a large screen.
Person A: Do you think it's worth upgrading to?
Person B: It depends on your needs and preferences.

PRACTICING UK ENGLISH

6.1 Role-Playing and Mock Conversations

Each conversation is accompanied by an explanation or prompt to assist you in understanding and practicing different aspects of the English language.

Ordering Food at a Restaurant

Practice using restaurant vocabulary and ordering food.

Customer: Good evening. May I have a menu, please?
Waiter: Of course, here you go.
Customer: Thank you. I'd like to start with a Caesar salad, please.
Waiter: Sure, and for the main course?
Customer: I'll have the grilled salmon with steamed vegetables, please.
Waiter: Excellent choice. Anything else?
Customer: No, that'll be all. Thank you.

Making a Hotel Reservation

Practice making a hotel reservation over the phone.

Customer: Good afternoon. I'd like to make a reservation for two nights, please.
Receptionist: Certainly. When will you be arriving?
Customer: I'll be arriving on the 15th of July.
Receptionist: Okay. How many guests will be staying?
Customer: It's just me.
Receptionist: Great. We have a single room available. Can I have your name, please?

Meeting a Friend at a Café

Simulate a casual conversation with a friend at a café.

Person A: Hey! It's great to see you. How have you been?
Person B: I've been good, thanks. What about you?
Person A: I've been busy with work, but I'm doing well overall. What can I get you to drink?
Person B: I'll have a cappuccino, please.
Person A: Alright, I'll order that for you.

Asking for Directions

Learn how to ask for and give directions.

Tourist: Excuse me, could you tell me how to get to the nearest subway station?
Local: Sure. Walk straight ahead for two blocks, then turn left. It'll be on your right.
Tourist: Thank you. Is it far from here?
Local: No, it's just a five-minute walk from here.

Talking about Hobbies

Discussing personal interests and hobbies.

Person A: So, what do you like to do in your free time?
Person B: I'm really into photography. I love capturing beautiful moments.
Person A: That's cool. How did you get into photography?
Person B: I started taking pictures with my smartphone, and then I bought a proper camera.

PRACTICING UK ENGLISH

Shopping for Clothes
Practice vocabulary related to clothing and shopping.

Shopper: Excuse me, where can I find the men's section?
Shop Assistant: It's on the second floor. Just take the escalator up, and you'll see it on your left.
Shopper: Thank you. I'm looking for a pair of jeans. Do you have any in a dark wash?
Shop Assistant: Yes, we do. Follow me, please.

Discussing Weekend Plans

Engage in a conversation about upcoming weekend activities.

Person A: Any plans for the weekend?
Person B: I'm thinking of going hiking with some friends. What about you?
Person A: I might check out that new art exhibition at the museum.

Describing a Recent Trip

Share details about a recent trip or vacation.

Person A: How was your trip to Paris?
Person B: It was amazing! The Eiffel Tower was breathtaking, and the Louvre was incredible.
Person A: Did you try any French cuisine?
Person B: Yes, I had escargot for the first time. It was surprisingly delicious.

Renting an Apartment

Practice conversations related to renting an apartment.

Renter: Hi, I'm interested in renting the apartment listed online.
Landlord: Great. It's a two-bedroom apartment with a spacious living room and a balcony.
Renter: How much is the monthly rent?
Landlord: It's £1,200 per month, excluding utilities.

Talking about Future Plans

Discussing long-term goals and future plans.

Person A: What are your plans for the future?
Person B: I'm planning to pursue a master's degree in computer science.
Person A: That sounds ambitious. Which university are you considering?
Person B: I'm looking at Imperial College, London and Cambridge.

Talking about Weather

Engaging in a conversation about the weather.

Person A: It's so hot today, isn't it?
Person B: Definitely. I wish it would rain and cool things down a bit.
Person A: I heard it might rain tomorrow. Let's hope for some relief.

PRACTICING UK ENGLISH

6.1 Role-Playing and Mock Conversations

Discussing Health and Fitness

Talking about maintaining a healthy lifestyle.

Person A: I've been trying to eat healthier and exercise regularly.
Person B: That's fantastic. What kind of exercises are you doing?
Person A: I've been going to the gym and doing a combination of cardio and weight training.

Discussing Travel Experiences

Sharing memorable travel experiences.

Person A: Have you ever been backpacking through Europe?
Person B: Yes, I travelled to several countries and met interesting people along the way.
Person A: Which country was your favourite?
Person B: It's hard to choose, but I really enjoyed my time in Italy.

Talking about Books

Discussing favourite books or literary genres.

Person A: Do you enjoy reading?
Person B: Yes, I love getting lost in a good book.
Person A: What genre do you prefer?
Person B: I'm a fan of mystery novels, but I also enjoy historical fiction.

Discussing Current Events

Engaging in a conversation about recent news or events.

Person A: Have you been following the news lately?
Person B: Yes, there have been a lot of interesting developments in the political landscape.
Person A: What's your opinion on the recent economic reforms?
Person B: It's a complex issue, but I think it's a step in the right direction.

Talking about Education

Discussing educational experiences and aspirations.

Person A: What are you studying in college?
Person B: I'm pursuing a degree in psychology.
Person A: That's fascinating. What made you interested in that field?
Person B: I've always been intrigued by human behaviour and the mind.

Discussing Cultural Differences

Talking about cultural practices and customs.

Person A: Have you noticed any cultural differences between your home country and the one you're in now?
Person B: Yes, there are quite a few differences in terms of food, greetings, and social norms.
Person A: Can you give me an example?
Person B: In my home country, it's customary to take off your shoes before entering someone's house.

PRACTICING UK ENGLISH

6.1 Role-Playing and Mock Conversations

Talking about Music

Discussing musical preferences and favourite genres.

Person A: What kind of music do you enjoy listening to?
Person B: I have a varied taste, but I particularly like rock and jazz.
Person A: Do you have any favourite bands or artists?
Person B: I'm a big fan of Led Zeppelin and Miles Davis.

Discussing Environmental Issues

Engaging in a conversation about environmental concerns.
Person A: Climate change has been a pressing issue lately.
Person B: Absolutely. We need to take action to protect our planet.
Person A: What do you think individuals can do to make a difference?
Person B: Small changes, like reducing plastic waste and conserving energy, can have a significant impact.

Talking about Sports

Discussing favourite sports and sporting events.
Person A: Did you watch the soccer match last night?
Person B: Yes, it was an intense game. The teams were evenly matched.
Person A: Who do you think will win the championship this year?
Person B: It's hard to say, but I have my bets on the defending champions.

Discussing Social Media

Talking about the impact of social media on society.
Person A: Social media seems to be playing a big role in our lives these days.
Person B: It's true. It has changed the way we communicate and share information.
Person A: What are your thoughts on the positive and negative effects of social media?
Person B: While it can be a great tool for connecting people, it also has its downsides, like addiction and privacy concerns.

Talking about Career Goals

Discussing long-term career aspirations.

Person A: Where do you see yourself in five years in terms of your career?
Person B: I'm hoping to be in a leadership position, overseeing a team of professionals.
Person A: What steps are you taking to achieve that goal?
Person B: I'm actively seeking opportunities for professional development and taking on additional responsibilities.

PRACTICING UK ENGLISH

6.1 Role-Playing and Mock Conversations

Discussing Art and Creativity

Talking about different forms of art and creative expression.

Person A: Are you into art?
Person B: Yes, I find art to be a great source of inspiration and self-expression.
Person A: What type of art do you enjoy the most?
Person B: I'm particularly drawn to abstract paintings and contemporary sculptures.

Talking about Personal Goals

Discussing personal goals and aspirations.

Person A: What are some goals you've set for yourself?
Person B: One of my goals is to learn a new language within the next year.
Person A: That's impressive. Which language are you interested in learning?
Person B: I'm considering either Spanish or Mandarin.

Talking about Volunteer Work

Discussing experiences and benefits of volunteering.

Person A: Do you engage in any volunteer work?
Person B: Yes, I volunteer at a local animal shelter every weekend.
Person A: What motivated you to get involved in volunteering?
Person B: I have always had a passion for animals and wanted to contribute to their well-being.

Discussing Fashion and Style

Talking about personal fashion choices and trends.

Person A: How would you describe your fashion sense?
Person B: I like to experiment with different styles, but I lean towards a more casual and comfortable look.
Person A: Do you follow any fashion trends?
Person B: I keep an eye on trends, but I prefer to wear what makes me feel confident and comfortable.

Talking about Technology in Education

Discussing the integration of technology in education.

Person A: Technology has revolutionised the way we learn.
Person B: Absolutely. It has made education more accessible and interactive.
Person A: What are some examples of technology used in classrooms?
Person B: Smartboards, online learning platforms, and educational apps are some common examples

Discussing Personal Achievements

Sharing personal achievements and milestones.
Person A: Have you accomplished anything significant recently?
Person B: Yes, I recently completed my first marathon.
Person A: That's impressive. How was the experience?
Person B: It was challenging, but crossing the finish line was incredibly rewarding.

PRACTICING UK ENGLISH

6.1 Role-Playing and Mock Conversations

Discussing Personal Interests and Hobbies

Sharing hobbies and discussing their significance.

Person A: What do you do in your free time?
Person B: I'm really into playing the guitar. It's a great way to unwind and express myself creatively.
Person A: How long have you been playing the guitar?
Person B: I've been playing for about five years now.

Discussing Healthy Eating Habits

Talking about the importance of maintaining a healthy diet.

Person A: How do you ensure you have a healthy diet?
Person B: I make sure to include a variety of fruits, vegetables, and whole grains in my meals.
Person A: Do you follow any specific diet plan?
Person B: I don't follow a specific plan, but I try to make mindful choices and listen to my body's needs.

Discussing the Importance of Physical Exercise

Talking about the benefits of regular physical exercise.

Person A: How often do you exercise?
Person B: I try to exercise at least three to four times a week.
Person A: What benefits have you noticed from regular exercise?
Person B: I have more energy, improved strength and endurance, and it helps me manage stress better.

Talking about Technology Addiction

Discussing the impact of technology addiction on individuals.

Person A: Technology addiction seems to be a growing concern.
Person B: Absolutely. It's important to find a healthy balance between technology use and other aspects of life.
Person A: How do you manage your own technology usage?
Person B: I try to set boundaries and allocate specific times for unplugging and engaging in other activities.

Talking about Time Management

Discussing strategies for effective time management.

Person A: How do you manage your time effectively?
Person B: I find creating to-do lists and prioritising tasks to be helpful.
Person A: Do you have any tips for avoiding procrastination?
Person B: Breaking tasks into smaller, manageable steps and setting deadlines can help overcome procrastination.

Talking about the Benefits of Traveling

Discussing the advantages of traveling and exploring new places.

Person A: What do you think are the benefits of traveling?
Person B: It exposes you to different cultures, broadens your perspective, and creates memorable experiences.
Person A: How often do you travel?
Person B: I try to travel at least once or twice a year to new destinations.

PRACTICING UK ENGLISH

6.1 Role-Playing and Mock Conversations

Discussing the Impact of Climate Change

Talking about the consequences of climate change and the importance of environmental conservation.

Person A: Climate change is a pressing issue. What are your thoughts on it?
Person B: It's a global concern that requires urgent action to mitigate its impact and preserve our planet.
Person A: What can individuals do to contribute to environmental conservation?
Person B: Adopting sustainable practices like reducing waste, conserving energy, and supporting eco-friendly initiatives can make a difference.

Talking about the Benefits of Volunteering Abroad

Discussing the advantages of participating in volunteer programs abroad.

Person A: What are the benefits of volunteering abroad?
Person B: It allows you to immerse yourself in a different culture, gain a global perspective, and make a positive impact.
Person A: Have you ever participated in a volunteer program abroad?
Person B: Yes, I volunteered in a rural community in Africa, and it was a transformative experience.

Discussing Financial Planning and Budgeting

Talking about the importance of financial planning and budgeting.

Person A: How do you manage your finances?
Person B: I create a monthly budget and track my expenses to ensure I'm saving and spending responsibly.
Person A: Do you have any tips for saving money?
Person B: Automating savings, avoiding impulse purchases, and comparing prices before making big purchases can help save money.

Talking about Personal Finance Goals

Discussing financial goals and strategies for achieving them.

Person A: What are your long-term financial goals?
Person B: I aim to be debt-free, save for retirement, and invest in real estate.
Person A: How do you plan to achieve those goals?
Person B: I budget carefully, seek financial advice, and continuously educate myself about investment opportunities.

PRACTICING UK ENGLISH

6.1 Role-Playing and Mock Conversations

Discussing the Role of Education in Society

Talking about the significance of education in personal and societal development.

Person A: What is the role of education in society?
Person B: Education equips individuals with knowledge, skills, and critical thinking abilities, leading to personal growth and societal progress.
Person A: Do you think formal education is the only path to success?
Person B: Not necessarily. While formal education is valuable, alternative paths like vocational training and entrepreneurship can also lead to success.

Talking about the Impact of Social Media on Relationships

Discussing the influence of social media on interpersonal relationships.

Person A: How do you think social media affects relationships?
Person B: Social media can both enhance and strain relationships. It depends on how it is used.
Person A: What are some challenges posed by social media in relationships?
Person B: Comparison, excessive screen time, and miscommunication can be challenges in maintaining healthy relationships.

Discussing the Impact of Technology on Communication

Talking about how technology has revolutionised communication.

Person A: How has technology changed the way we communicate?
Person B: It has made communication faster, more accessible, and enabled us to connect with people from all over the world.
Person A: Do you think face-to-face communication is still important?
Person B: Absolutely. While technology facilitates communication, nothing can replace the depth and nuances of in-person interactions.

Discussing the Importance of Mental Health

Talking about the significance of mental health awareness.

Person A: Mental health has gained more attention in recent years.
Person B: Yes, it's essential to prioritise mental well-being and reduce the stigma surrounding mental health.
Person A: What are some self-care practices you engage in for your mental health?
Person B: I practice mindfulness meditation and engage in activities that bring me joy and relaxation.

PRACTICING UK ENGLISH

6.1 Role-Playing and Mock Conversations

Talking about the Role of Arts and Humanities in Society

Discussing the significance of arts and humanities in society.

Person A: What is the role of arts and humanities in society?
Person B: Arts and humanities enrich our lives, foster creativity, promote empathy, and provide critical insights into human experiences.
Person A: Do you think society values arts and humanities enough?
Person B: There is room for improvement. It's important to recognise and support the arts for their cultural and societal contributions.

Talking about the Advantages of Learning a Second Language

Discussing the benefits of being bilingual or multilingual.

Person A: What are the advantages of learning a second language?
Person B: It broadens your cultural understanding, improves cognitive skills, and opens up more job opportunities.
Person A: Which languages do you think are valuable to learn?
Person B: It depends on your goals, but languages like English, Spanish, Mandarin, and French are widely spoken globally.

CHAPTER VII

PRACTICE ACTIVITIES FOR ADVANCED ENGLISH LEARNERS

CHAPTER SEVEN

PRACTICE ACTIVITIES

Activity 1: Professional Email Writing

Objective: Improve formal writing skills and appropriate tone for professional communication.

Scenario: Write an email to a colleague requesting a meeting to discuss a project update.

Steps:

1. **Greeting:**
   - Example: "Dear [Colleague's Name],"
2. **Introduction and Purpose:**
   - Example: "I hope this email finds you well. I am writing to request a meeting to discuss the latest updates on our current project."
3. **Detail the Request:**
   - Example: "Specifically, I would like to go over the recent developments in the marketing strategy and address any concerns you might have."
4. **Propose a Time and Date:**
   - Example: "Could we possibly schedule a meeting for next Tuesday at 2 PM? If this time does not work for you, please let me know your availability."
5. **Closing:**
   - Example: "Thank you for your time, and I look forward to our discussion."
   - Example: "Best regards, [Your Name]"

Tips:
- Use polite and formal language.
- Be clear and concise.
- Make sure the purpose of the email is easily understood.

CHAPTER SEVEN

PRACTICE ACTIVITIES

Activity 2: Networking at a Professional Event

Objective: Practice initiating and maintaining professional conversations.

Scenario: Attend a networking event and introduce yourself to a new contact.

Steps:

1. **Introduction:**
   - Example: "Hello, my name is [Your Name]. I work as a [Your Job Title] at [Your Company]."
2. **Small Talk:**
   - Example: "How are you finding the event so far?"
   - Example: "Have you attended similar events before?"
3. **Finding Common Ground:**
   - Example: "I noticed you mentioned you're in the tech industry. What specific projects are you working on currently?"
   - Example: "I read an interesting article recently about the latest trends in our field. Have you come across it?"
4. **Exchanging Contact Information:**
   - Example: "It was great chatting with you. Would you be interested in exchanging contact information to stay in touch?"
5. **Closing the Conversation:**
   - Example: "Thank you for the conversation. I look forward to connecting with you soon."

Tips:
- Maintain eye contact and use open body language.
- Listen actively and show interest in the other person's work.
- Have a few topics of conversation ready to avoid awkward pauses.

CHAPTER SEVEN

PRACTICE ACTIVITIES

Activity 3: Social Interaction at a Dinner Party

Objective: Enhance conversational skills in a social setting.

Scenario: Engage in a conversation at a dinner party with new acquaintances.

Steps:

1. **Introduction:**
   - Example: "Hi, I'm [Your Name]. It's nice to meet you."
2. **Small Talk:**
   - Example: "How do you know the host?"
   - Example: "Have you tried the appetisers? They are delicious."
3. **Sharing Personal Interests:**
   - Example: "I love traveling. Recently, I visited [Destination]. Have you been there?"
   - Example: "In my free time, I enjoy reading. What about you?"
4. **Keeping the Conversation Going:**
   - Example: "That sounds fascinating. Can you tell me more about it?"
   - Example: "I've always wanted to learn more about [Topic]. What would you recommend for a beginner?"
5. **Closing the Conversation:**
   - Example: "It's been lovely talking with you. I hope we can continue our conversation later."

Tips:
- Ask open-ended questions to encourage discussion.
- Share personal experiences and interests.
- Be polite and show enthusiasm in your responses.

CHAPTER SEVEN

PRACTICE ACTIVITIES

Activity 4: Giving a Professional Presentation

Objective: Improve public speaking and presentation skills.

Scenario: Deliver a presentation on a new project proposal to your team.

Steps:

1. **Opening:**
   - Example: "Good morning, everyone. Thank you for being here today. I am excited to present our new project proposal."
2. **Introduction:**
   - Example: "To start, I will give a brief overview of the project's objectives and goals."
3. **Main Content:**
   - Example: "First, let's discuss the market analysis. We have identified a significant opportunity in..."
   - Example: "Next, I will outline the proposed strategy and timeline for implementation."
4. **Visual Aids:**
   - Example: "As you can see on this slide, the projected growth is significant."
   - Example: "This chart illustrates our expected milestones over the next six months."
5. **Conclusion:**
   - Example: "In conclusion, this project has the potential to drive substantial growth for our company."
   - Example: "I am open to any questions or feedback you may have."
6. **Q&A Session:**
   - Example: "Thank you for your attention. I will now take any questions you may have."

Tips:
- Practice your presentation multiple times.
- Use clear and concise language.
- Engage your audience with eye contact and body language.

CHAPTER SEVEN

PRACTICE ACTIVITIES

Activity 5: Participating in a Team Meeting

Objective: Practice collaborative discussion and decision-making.

Scenario: Take part in a team meeting to brainstorm ideas for a new project.

Steps:

1. **Opening:**
   - Example: "Thank you all for joining today. Let's start by reviewing our main objectives for this brainstorming session."
2. **Contributing Ideas:**
   - Example: "One idea I have is to leverage social media for our marketing campaign."
   - Example: "What if we introduced a referral program to increase customer engagement?"
3. **Building on Others' Ideas:**
   - Example: "I like that idea, and I think we could also add a loyalty program to complement it."
   - Example: "That's a great point. Additionally, we could consider..."
4. **Clarifying and Asking Questions:**
   - Example: "Can you elaborate on how that strategy would work?"
   - Example: "What resources would we need to implement this idea?"
5. **Summarising and Reaching Consensus:**
   - Example: "To summarise, we have several promising ideas: social media marketing, a referral program, and a loyalty program."
   - Example: "Let's take a vote on which idea to prioritise first."

Tips:
- Be respectful and open to others' ideas.
- Provide constructive feedback.
- Ensure everyone has a chance to contribute.

CHAPTER SEVEN

PRACTICE ACTIVITIES

Activity 6: Negotiating a Business Deal

Objective: Develop negotiation skills and language for business contexts.

Scenario: Role-play a negotiation session between two parties discussing a potential business deal.

Steps:

1. **Setting the Stage:**
   - Example: "Welcome to our negotiation session. Today, we will discuss the terms of the proposed partnership."
2. **Stating Positions:**
   - Example: "Our company is looking for a mutually beneficial agreement that meets our objectives."
   - Example: "We are interested in exploring opportunities for collaboration but have specific requirements."
3. **Exploring Interests:**
   - Example: "What are your main priorities and objectives for this partnership?"
   - Example: "We are keen to understand how we can align our goals to create value for both parties."
4. **Making Offers and Counteroffers:**
   - Example: "We propose a revenue-sharing model with a 50/50 split."
   - Example: "Could you consider adjusting the terms to include additional incentives for early adoption?"
5. **Finding Common Ground:**
   - Example: "It seems we both value transparency and communication in our partnerships."
   - Example: "Perhaps we can agree on a trial period to test the effectiveness of our collaboration."
6. **Reaching Agreement:**
   - Example: "After careful consideration, we are prepared to accept your revised proposal."
   - Example: "We believe this agreement aligns with our objectives and will lead to a successful partnership."

Tips:
- Maintain professionalism and focus on the issue at hand.
- Listen actively and show understanding of the other party's perspective.
- Aim for a win-win outcome where both parties benefit.

CHAPTER SEVEN

PRACTICE ACTIVITIES

Activity 7: Role-Playing Customer Service Scenarios

Objective: Practice effective communication and problem-solving skills in customer service situations.

Scenario: Role-play various customer service scenarios, such as handling complaints or providing product recommendations.

Steps:

1. **Identifying the Issue:**
   - Example: "Hello, how may I assist you today?"
   - Example: "I understand you are experiencing an issue with your recent purchase. Could you please provide more details?"
2. **Empathising with the Customer:**
   - Example: "I'm sorry to hear about your experience. I can imagine how frustrating that must be."
   - Example: "Thank you for bringing this to our attention. Your feedback is valuable to us."
3. **Offering Solutions:**
   - Example: "Let me look into this issue for you and see how we can resolve it."
   - Example: "Would you like a replacement product, a refund, or store credit?"
4. **Resolving the Issue:**
   - Example: "I have processed a refund for the faulty item, and it should appear in your account within 3-5 business days."
   - Example: "We apologise for the inconvenience caused. As a gesture of goodwill, we would like to offer you a discount on your next purchase."
5. **Following Up:**
   - Example: "Is there anything else I can assist you with?"
   - Example: "Please feel free to contact us if you have any further questions or concerns."

Tips:

- Remain calm and composed, even in challenging situations.
- Use positive language and focus on finding solutions.
- Ensure the customer feels valued and heard throughout the interaction.

CHAPTER SEVEN

PRACTICE ACTIVITIES

Activity 8: Simulated Job Interviews

Objective: Practice interviewing skills and language for professional settings.

Scenario: Participate in mock job interviews, taking turns as both the interviewer and the interviewee.

Steps:
1. **Interviewer Preparation:**
    - Example: "As the interviewer, I will review the candidate's CV and prepare a list of questions."
2. **Candidate Introduction:**
    - Example: "Good morning, my name is [Your Name], and I am excited to be interviewing for the [Position Title] role."
3. **Answering Interview Questions:**
    - Example: "Can you tell me about a time when you faced a challenging situation at work and how you handled it?"
    - Example: "What skills and experience do you bring to this role that make you a strong candidate?"
4. **Asking Questions as the Interviewer:**
    - Example: "What motivated you to apply for this position?"
    - Example: "Can you provide an example of a successful project you led in your previous role?"
5. **Closing the Interview:**
    - Example: "Thank you for taking the time to interview with us today. We will be in touch regarding the next steps."
    - Example: "Is there anything else you would like to add before we conclude the interview?"

Tips:
- Prepare responses to common interview questions in advance.
- Showcase relevant skills and experiences that align with the job requirements.
- Practice active listening and maintain good posture and eye contact.

CHAPTER SEVEN
PRACTICE ACTIVITIES
Activity 9: Leading a Team Meeting

Objective: Develop leadership and facilitation skills in a professional setting.

Scenario: Facilitate a team meeting to discuss project updates and address any challenges or concerns.

Steps:
1. **Setting the Agenda:**
    - Example: "Good afternoon, everyone. Today's agenda includes a review of our project milestones, followed by a discussion on potential roadblocks."
2. **Reviewing Progress:**
    - Example: "Let's start by reviewing our progress against the project timeline. Can someone provide an update on the status of each deliverable?"
3. **Identifying Challenges:**
    - Example: "Are there any challenges or obstacles preventing us from meeting our goals? Let's address them openly and brainstorm solutions."
4. **Encouraging Participation:**
    - Example: "I encourage everyone to share their thoughts and ideas. We value your input and insights."
5. **Making Decisions:**
    - Example: "Based on our discussion, let's agree on the next steps and assign responsibilities accordingly."
    - Example: "Is everyone in agreement with the proposed approach? If not, let's discuss alternative solutions."
6. **Summarising Action Items:**
    - Example: "Before we adjourn, let's recap the action items and deadlines. Can someone volunteer to document the meeting minutes?"

Tips:
- Be prepared and organised with an agenda and supporting materials.
- Foster a collaborative and inclusive environment where everyone feels comfortable sharing their opinions.
- Ensure clear communication and follow-up on action items after the meeting.

CHAPTER SEVEN

PRACTICE ACTIVITIES

Activity 10: Giving a Persuasive Presentation

Objective: Practice persuasive communication skills to influence and persuade an audience.

Scenario: Deliver a presentation aimed at convincing stakeholders to support a new project proposal.

Steps:

1. **Setting the Stage:**
   a. Example "Good morning, everyone. Today, I am excited to present a new project proposal that has the potential to revolutionise our product line and significantly boost our market position."
   b. Example "Hello, everyone. I appreciate your time today as we discuss a project that could lead to significant innovation and growth for our company."

2. **Presenting the Proposal:**
   a. Example: "Our proposal centers around a new software solution that will streamline our internal processes, enhancing efficiency and reducing costs by 20% over the next year."
   b. Example: "This initiative aims to develop a cutting-edge mobile app designed to improve customer engagement and retention, targeting a 30% increase in user interaction."

3. **Highlighting Key Benefits:**
   a. Example: "By implementing this project, we anticipate a 25% reduction in operational costs, which will directly impact our bottom line."
   b. Example: "One of the major advantages is the projected 40% increase in customer satisfaction, as we will be addressing key pain points with our new service."

4. **Addressing Potential Concerns:**
   a. Example: "I understand there might be concerns regarding the project's upfront costs. However, our detailed financial analysis shows a break-even point within the first two years, followed by substantial profit margins."
   b. Example: "Some of you may be worried about the resource allocation. We have planned a phased approach that ensures minimal disruption to ongoing projects."

CHAPTER SEVEN

PRACTICE ACTIVITIES

Activity 10: Giving a Persuasive Presentation

5. Encouraging Feedback and Discussion:
- Example: "I encourage everyone to voice their thoughts and questions. Let's have an open discussion to ensure we address all concerns and optimise our plan."
- Example: "Your feedback is crucial. Let's discuss any reservations you may have and find solutions together. We value your insights and want to incorporate them into our strategy."

6. Building Consensus:
- Example 1: "Given the positive response, let's formalise our commitment to this project and outline the specific roles and responsibilities moving forward."
- Example 2: "It seems we have a consensus on the project's importance. Let's agree on a timeline and action plan to begin implementation as soon as possible."

7. Summarising Key Points and Action Items:
- Example 1: "To recap, the proposed project is expected to deliver significant financial and operational benefits. Our next steps include finalising the project charter and starting the initial phase by next month."
- Example 2: "In summary, this initiative promises to enhance our market presence and customer satisfaction. Let's assign key team members to lead the project and schedule our next meeting to track progress."

Tips:
- Know Your Audience: Tailor your message to address the interests and concerns of your audience.
- Use Data and Evidence: Support your arguments with solid data and real-world examples.
- Stay Confident and Clear: Maintain a confident tone and articulate your points clearly.
- Engage the Audience: Encourage participation and make the presentation interactive.
- Follow-Up: Ensure clear communication and follow-up on the agreed action items.

CHAPTER SEVEN

PRACTICE ACTIVITIES

6.2 Writing Exercises and Journaling

The key to improving your English through writing exercises and journaling is consistent practice. Have fun exploring these prompts and let your creativity soar!

Write a short story using at least five vocabulary words you recently learned.
Example: Once upon a time, in a quaint village nestled among the mountains, lived a peculiar creature called the "quizzical."

Describe your favourite place in nature using sensory details.
Example: The serene beach greeted me with the soft touch of warm sand beneath my feet, the gentle sound of waves crashing against the shore, and the refreshing scent of salty sea air.

Write a letter to your future self, reflecting on your goals and aspirations.
Example: Dear Future Me, I hope you have accomplished all the dreams we once held close to our heart.

Create a dialogue between two fictional characters discussing an important decision.
Example:
Character A: I don't know if I should take the job offer. It's a big decision.
Character B: Have you considered the potential opportunities it could bring?

Write a poem about a memorable childhood experience.
Example: In the backyard, laughter danced with the wind, as we chased dreams beneath the sun's golden rays.

Imagine you are a detective and write a crime-solving mystery story.
Example: Detective Johnson examined the crime scene, searching for any clues that could lead to the identity of the mysterious culprit.

Write a persuasive essay arguing for or against a controversial topic.
Example: The use of technology in classrooms enhances learning and prepares students for the digital age.

Describe your favourite food using vivid language.
Example: The velvety chocolate cake melted in my mouth, releasing a burst of rich, decadent Flavours.

Write a journal entry reflecting on a significant life event.
Example: Today marked a turning point in my life — an opportunity that unfolded unexpectedly, changing the trajectory of my journey.

CHAPTER SEVEN

PRACTICE ACTIVITIES

6.2 Writing Exercises and Journaling

Create a character profile for a fictional protagonist, including their background, personality, and goals.
Example: Name: Emily Walker | Background: Born and raised in a small town, Emily has always had a thirst for adventure and a desire to make a positive impact.

Write a travel blog post describing a dream destination you would like to visit.
Example: Welcome to the breathtaking landscapes and vibrant culture of the enchanting city of Prague.

Reflect on a book you recently read, discussing its themes and lessons.
Example: Through its intricate storytelling, the novel highlighted the power of resilience and the beauty of human connection.

Write a short script for a dialogue between two friends planning a surprise party.
Example:
Friend A: I think a beach party would be perfect! It's her favourite place.
Friend B: That's a great idea. Let's start organising the decorations and food.

Imagine you are a journalist reporting on a major news event and write an article about it.
Example: In a historic turn of events, scientists have made a groundbreaking discovery that could revolutionise the medical field.

Write a reflection on a meaningful quote and how it relates to your life.
Example: "The only way to do great work is to love what you do." - Steve Jobs. These words resonate deeply with me as I navigate my career path.

Write a letter to someone who has inspired you, expressing your gratitude.
Example: Dear Teacher, Your unwavering dedication and belief in my potential have shaped me into the person I am today.

Create a detailed plan for a personal project or goal you want to accomplish.
Example: Project: Learn to play the guitar | Goals: Practice for at least 30 minutes every day, take lessons from a professional guitarist, and perform at an open mic night.

Write a review of a movie or TV series you recently watched, sharing your thoughts and recommendations.
Example: The captivating storyline, stellar performances, and stunning cinematography make this film an absolute must-watch.

CHAPTER SEVEN

PRACTICE ACTIVITIES

6.2 Writing Exercises and Journaling

Imagine you are a character in your favourite book and write a diary entry from their perspective.
Example: Dear Diary, Today, I ventured into the unknown, following the path paved by destiny and embracing the challenges that lie ahead.

Write a letter to your future child, sharing your hopes and dreams for them.
Example: My dearest child, as I write this letter, my heart brims with unconditional love and boundless dreams for your future.

Describe a childhood memory that brings you joy, focusing on the sights, sounds, and emotions.
Example: The vibrant colours of the carousel, the infectious laughter of children, and the sheer excitement coursing through my veins — it was a moment frozen in time.

Write a poem inspired by a beautiful sunset.
Example: As the sun gracefully descended, painting the sky in hues of gold and crimson, nature whispered its lullaby, bidding the world goodnight.

Imagine you are a superhero with unique powers, and write a short story about a heroic adventure.
Example: With a single flick of my wrist, I summoned the power of lightning, ready to protect the city from imminent danger.

Reflect on a difficult challenge you faced and describe how you overcame it.
Example: It was an uphill battle, filled with setbacks and doubts, but with unwavering determination, I persevered and emerged stronger than ever.

Write a letter to your favourite author, expressing how their work has impacted your life.
Example: Dear [Author's Name], your words have woven themselves into the fabric of my being, igniting my imagination and touching my soul.

Describe a dream you had recently, exploring its symbolism and meaning.
Example: In the realm of dreams, I wandered through a labyrinth of mysteries, deciphering the hidden messages whispered by my subconscious.

Write a short story set in a dystopian future, depicting a world transformed by technology.
Example: In the not-so-distant future, humanity grappled with the consequences of its insatiable thirst for innovation.

CHAPTER SEVEN
PRACTICE ACTIVITIES
6.2 Writing Exercises and Journaling

Imagine you have the power to time travel, and write a journal entry about the historical period you would visit.
Example: Today, I found myself transported to the Renaissance — a time of artistic brilliance, intellectual exploration, and cultural revolution.

Write a letter of appreciation to a person who has positively impacted your life.
Example: Dear [Person's Name], your unwavering support and belief in me have been a guiding light in my darkest moments.

Create a short story using a dialogue-only format, focusing on the character's emotions and intentions.
Example:
Character A: Why did you do it?
Character B: I had no choice. It was the only way to protect those I love.

Reflect on a quote about resilience and describe a time when you demonstrated resilience in your own life.
Example: "Life doesn't get easier or more forgiving; we get stronger and more resilient." – Steve Maraboli. This quote resonates deeply with me, as I recall a time when I faced overwhelming challenges.

Write a letter to your younger self, offering advice and words of encouragement.
Example: Dear Younger Me, as you embark on this journey called life, remember that every obstacle you encounter is an opportunity for growth.

Describe a favourite childhood toy or object that holds sentimental value for you.
Example: Tucked away in the corner of my room, amidst the dust and memories, lies my treasured teddy bear — a silent guardian of cherished moments.

Write a poem inspired by the beauty of nature, focusing on a specific element like a blooming flower or a glistening river.
Example: Ode to the Rose, whose petals unfurl like delicate whispers, captivating hearts with your ethereal beauty.

Imagine you are an inventor and describe a groundbreaking invention you would create.
Example: Introducing the Time-Sync Chronometer — a device that harnesses the power of time itself, allowing seamless travel across different eras.

Reflect on a personal setback or failure and discuss the lessons you learned from it.
Example: In the depths of failure, I discovered resilience, humility, and the strength to rise again.

CHAPTER SEVEN

PRACTICE ACTIVITIES

6.2 Writing Exercises and Journaling

Write a dialogue between two historical figures discussing their contrasting viewpoints.

Example:

Historical Figure A: Our people deserve freedom and equality.

Historical Figure B: But at what cost? We must consider the consequences of our actions.

Describe a favourite childhood book and explain why it holds a special place in your heart.

Example: The worn pages of this cherished book hold within them a portal to whimsical realms, sparking my imagination and nurturing my love for storytelling.

Write a short story from the perspective of an animal, exploring their thoughts and experiences.

Example: Through the eyes of the majestic eagle, I soared through boundless skies, witnessing the beauty and chaos of the world below.

Reflect on a memorable journey you took, describing the sights, sounds, and people you encountered.

Example: As I ventured through the winding streets of an ancient city, I discovered a kaleidoscope of cultures, each painting its unique strokes upon the canvas of my soul.

Write a letter to a future generation, sharing your hopes for a better world.

Example: Dear Future Generation, as you inherit the torch of humanity, may you illuminate the path towards compassion, understanding, and sustainable harmony.

Describe a piece of artwork that resonates with you, interpreting its symbolism and emotions.

Example: The masterpiece before me whispered a silent symphony, evoking emotions buried deep within my soul—a testament to the power of art.

Write a poem expressing gratitude for the simple joys in life, like a warm cup of tea or a gentle breeze.

Example: In the whispers of a tranquil morning, I find solace—grateful for the fleeting moments that awaken my senses and fill my heart with gratitude.

CHAPTER SEVEN

PRACTICE ACTIVITIES

6.2 Writing Exercises and Journaling

Reflect on a mentor or role model who has guided you on your journey, describing the impact they have had on your life.
Example: Like a lighthouse amidst the stormy seas, you guided me with unwavering support and illuminated the path to self-discovery.

Write a short story set in a futuristic society, exploring the consequences of advanced technology on human existence.
Example: In a world intertwined with artificial intelligence, humanity teetered on the precipice of its own creation.

Imagine you are an explorer discovering a hidden treasure, and describe the moment of revelation.
Example: As I brushed away the layers of dust, the glimmering treasure emerged — a symbol of untold stories and forgotten dreams.

Reflect on a personal mantra or motto that guides your actions and decisions.
Example: "Embrace the unknown, for it holds the key to growth and transformation." This mantra reminds me to embrace uncertainty and lean into the opportunities it presents.

Write a letter to someone you have lost, expressing your feelings and memories.
Example: Dear [Person's Name], though you are no longer with us, your presence lingers, etched forever in the tapestry of our shared experiences.

Describe a dream career you aspire to have, outlining the steps you would take to achieve it.
Example: From the depths of my imagination, I envision a career where I can intertwine creativity, purpose, and impact — a path paved with passion and unwavering dedication.

Write a reflection on the power of kindness and how small acts of compassion can transform lives.
Example: Like ripples in a tranquil pond, kindness reverberates through the tapestry of existence, awakening hearts and igniting a chain of love and empathy.

CHAPTER SEVEN
PRACTICE ACTIVITIES

6.3 Using Idioms and Expressions in Speech

Using idioms and expressions in speech can add colour and depth to your language and make your conversations more engaging. When learning English and using idioms and expressions in speech, here are some helpful tips:

1. Start with common idioms: Begin by learning and practicing commonly used idioms and expressions in everyday conversations. These idioms will be more familiar to native speakers and easier to incorporate into your speech.
2. Study their meanings and usage: Take the time to understand the meanings, origins, and appropriate contexts for each idiom or expression you come across. Use reliable resources such as dictionaries, textbooks, or online language learning platforms to learn about their usage.
3. Listen and observe: Pay attention to how native English speakers use idioms and expressions in various situations. Listen to conversations, watch movies, TV shows, and videos to gain exposure to their natural usage.
4. Practice in context: Practice using idioms and expressions in appropriate contexts. Role-play different scenarios, engage in conversations with native English speakers, or join language exchange groups to receive feedback on your usage.
5. Start with simpler idioms: Begin with simpler idioms and expressions that are more commonly used. Gradually expand your repertoire as you become more comfortable and confident in their application.
6. Learn idioms related to specific topics: Explore idioms and expressions that are relevant to specific topics you're interested in or that you frequently encounter. For example, if you're learning English for business, focus on business-related idioms.
7. Use idioms in writing and speaking exercises: Incorporate idioms and expressions into your writing and speaking exercises. This will help you practice using them in context and reinforce your understanding of their meanings.
8. Seek feedback and corrections: Don't be afraid to ask for feedback from native English speakers or your language instructor. They can help you identify any errors or suggest improvements in your usage of idioms and expressions.
9. Be patient and persistent: Learning idioms and expressions takes time and practice. Be patient with yourself and keep practicing consistently. Over time, you will become more comfortable and fluent in using them naturally.

CHAPTER SEVEN
PRACTICE ACTIVITIES

6.3 Using Idioms and Expressions in Speech

Remember, idioms and expressions add richness to your language, but it's important to use them appropriately and with a good understanding of their meanings. Practice regularly, seek opportunities to apply them, and enjoy the process of learning and incorporating idioms and expressions into your English speech.

Here are some tips on how to effectively use idioms and expressions:

1. Understand the meaning: Idioms and expressions often have figurative meanings that may not be immediately apparent. Take the time to understand the underlying meaning of an idiom or expression before using it.
2. Context is key: Use idioms and expressions in appropriate contexts where they make sense. Consider the topic, the people you're speaking to, and the overall tone of the conversation. Select idioms and expressions that fit well within the context.
3. Be mindful of formality: Idioms and expressions can vary in formality. Some are suitable for casual conversations, while others are more appropriate for formal or professional settings. Adapt your choice of idioms and expressions to match the level of formality required.
4. Use idioms sparingly: While idioms can enhance your speech, using too many of them can make your language sound unnatural or confusing. Incorporate idioms and expressions strategically, using them to emphasise a point or add flair to your speech.
5. Provide context when necessary: If you're using an idiom or expression that might not be familiar to everyone in the conversation, provide a brief explanation or example to help others understand its meaning.
6. Practice and exposure: Regularly expose yourself to idioms and expressions by reading books, articles, or listening to native speakers. This will expand your knowledge and understanding of their usage, allowing you to incorporate them more naturally into your speech.
7. Pay attention to feedback: Observe how others react to your use of idioms and expressions. If they seem confused or ask for clarification, it might indicate that you need to adjust your usage or provide more context.

Remember, using idioms and expressions should enhance your communication, but clarity and understanding should always be your primary goal.

CHAPTER SEVEN

PRACTICE ACTIVITIES

6.4 Receiving Feedback and Corrections

When learning English, asking for feedback and corrections is crucial for improvement. Here are effective ways to ask for feedback and corrections:

- "Could you please review this sentence and let me know if it's grammatically correct?" - This straightforward request asks for specific feedback on the grammatical accuracy of a sentence.

- "I'm trying to improve my English writing skills. Can you provide feedback on this paragraph?" - This statement conveys your intention to enhance your writing skills and asks for feedback on a specific paragraph.

- "Would you mind pointing out any errors or awkward phrases in my speech?" - By asking for errors and awkward phrases in your spoken English, you invite the listener to provide feedback for improvement.

- "I'm working on my pronunciation. Could you listen to me and tell me if I'm saying these words correctly?" - This request focuses on pronunciation improvement and seeks confirmation on the accurate pronunciation of specific words.

- "Can you correct any mistakes you find in this email I drafted?" - By asking for corrections in an email, you demonstrate a willingness to learn and improve your written English skills..

CHAPTER SEVEN

PRACTICE ACTIVITIES

6.4 Receiving Feedback and Corrections

- "I'm trying to expand my vocabulary. Is there a better word I could use in this sentence?" - This question indicates your desire to enhance your vocabulary and asks for suggestions for more appropriate word choices in each sentence.

- "I'm practicing English conversation. Could you let me know if my sentence structure is accurate?" - By requesting feedback on sentence structure during a conversation, you express your dedication to improving your spoken English.

- "Would you be willing to proofread this essay and suggest any necessary changes?" - This polite inquiry seeks assistance in proofreading an essay, indicating your commitment to producing high-quality written work.

- "I want to improve my English fluency. Can you provide feedback on my speaking speed and clarity?" - By seeking feedback on fluency, speaking speed, and clarity, you demonstrate your goal of becoming a more fluent English speaker.

- "I'm having trouble with prepositions. Could you correct any mistakes in this sentence?" - This request targets a specific grammar area and asks for help in identifying and correcting errors related to prepositions.

- "Could you point out any errors in my use of tenses in this paragraph?" - By seeking feedback on tense usage in a paragraph, you show a willingness to improve your grasp of English grammar.

CHAPTER SEVEN

PRACTICE ACTIVITIES

6.4 Receiving Feedback and Corrections

- "I'm working on my writing style. Can you provide suggestions to make it more engaging?" - This request seeks advice on improving writing style to make it more captivating and indicates your dedication to developing your writing skills.

- "Would you be able to identify any pronunciation errors I might be making?" - By asking for assistance in identifying pronunciation errors, you express your eagerness to refine your spoken English.

- "I'm trying to improve my English comprehension. Could you provide feedback on my understanding of this text?" - This request asks for feedback on comprehension skills, emphasising your commitment to better understand written English material.

- "Can you correct any grammatical mistakes you find in this short story I wrote?" - By asking for grammatical corrections in a short story, you display a desire to improve your writing accuracy and storytelling abilities.

- "I'm practicing giving presentations in English. Can you evaluate my delivery and provide suggestions?" - This request asks for feedback on presentation skills, seeking evaluation and suggestions to enhance your English presentation abilities.

CHAPTER SEVEN

PRACTICE ACTIVITIES

6.4 Receiving Feedback and Corrections

- "Could you please correct any errors in my use of articles (a, an, the) in this paragraph?" - This request targets the proper usage of articles, specifically asking for corrections in a given paragraph.

- "I'm working on my listening skills. Could you provide feedback on my understanding of this audio clip?" - By asking for feedback on listening skills based on an audio clip, you demonstrate your commitment to improving comprehension abilities in spoken English.

- "I'm studying English idioms. Can you correct any mistakes I made in using them in this sentence?" - This request seeks corrections related to the use of English idioms, highlighting your efforts to learn and apply idiomatic expressions accurately.

- "I'm trying to improve my English overall. Can you give me any general feedback or suggestions?" - This open-ended request invites general feedback and suggestions to improve your English skills as a whole.

Remember, when asking for feedback and corrections, it's important to be respectful, appreciative, and receptive to the guidance provided by others.

GOLDEN SIX

Significantly reduce the chances of being immediately identified as foreign, and integrate more smoothly into English-speaking environments by focusing on the six elements below:

Accent and Pronunciation

- Accent Reduction: Work on minimizing a strong native accent by mimicking the intonation, rhythm, and sounds of native English speakers.
- Clear Pronunciation: Focus on accurately pronouncing words, especially tricky sounds like "th," "r," and "l," which can reveal non-native speech.

Vocabulary and Word Choice

- Varied Vocabulary: Use a wide range of vocabulary, including synonyms and nuanced words, rather than sticking to basic, overused terms.
- Avoiding Over-Formal or Stilted Language: Use everyday language rather than overly formal or textbook English, which can make speech sound unnatural.

Fluency and Natural Speech Patterns

- Smooth Speech: Practice speaking without long pauses, fillers, or hesitations to create a more fluent and confident delivery.
- Use of Idioms and Colloquialisms: Incorporate common idioms, slang, and colloquial expressions that native speakers use in everyday conversation.
- Understanding Contractions and Reductions: Use contractions (e.g., "don't" instead of "do not") and reductions (e.g., "gonna" instead of "going to") naturally, as these are common in native speech.

Confidence and Delivery

- Confident Communication: Speak with confidence, maintaining appropriate volume, pace, and clarity.
- Active Listening: Show understanding by responding naturally and appropriately in conversations, picking up on cues that a native speaker would recognise.

Grammar and Syntax

- Correct Sentence Structure: Use the correct word order and grammar rules typical of English, avoiding structures from their native language that might sound unnatural in English.
- Mastering Tenses and Verb Forms: Accurately use tenses, verb forms, and other grammatical structures that native speakers intuitively understand.

Cultural Awareness and Contextual Understanding

- Cultural References: Be familiar with cultural references, humour, and the context behind certain phrases or idioms to use them appropriately.
- Non-Verbal Communication: Understand and use body language, gestures, and eye contact in ways that align with English-speaking norms.

CONCLUSION
SO, WHAT WILL YOU DO NOW?

Learning a language to an advanced level requires dedication, consistency, and effective methods to help you learn English to an advanced level quickly here are some summary reminders:

   Surround yourself with the language as much as possible. Change your phone, computer, social media, and even entertainment settings to UK English language. Listen to music, watch movies, and read books in UK English.
   Dedicate a specific amount of time daily to practicing the language. Regularity is key to retaining and improving your skills.
   Engage in conversation as much as possible. You can find language exchange partners, hire a tutor, or even practice speaking to yourself. This helps you apply what you've learned and improves your fluency.
   If possible, visit a region where British English is spoken. Immersion programs can accelerate your learning by forcing you to use the language in real-life situations.

Note: This book provides an overview and guidance on UK jargon, colloquialisms, and idioms, but it is important to remember that language is fluid and constantly evolving. Regional variations and personal expressions may not be fully captured within these pages. The reader is encouraged to embrace the living language and continue exploring and engaging with British English in real-life contexts.

WHAT I WILL DO NOW

Listen to podcasts, news, or watch videos in the target language. Try to understand the context even if you don't catch every word. This trains your ears and helps with comprehension.

Start with simple texts and gradually move to more complex materials. This improves your vocabulary, grammar, and understanding of idiomatic expressions.

Language learning takes time. Don't get discouraged by mistakes or slow progress. Stay positive and celebrate your achievements along the way.

There are many language learning apps available, such as Duolingo, Babbel, Rosetta Stone, and more. These apps make learning interactive and engaging.

While immersion is important, understanding grammar rules is also crucial. Invest time in understanding the grammar structure of the language.

Define your language learning goals, both short-term and long-term. This keeps you motivated and gives you a clear direction.

Online forums, social media groups, and local meetups dedicated to the language can provide you with a supportive community and opportunities to practice.

Use flashcards or spaced repetition systems to reinforce vocabulary. Apps like Anki or Quislet can help you with this.

Keep a journal or write short essays in the target language. Writing helps reinforce what you've learned and improves your ability to express yourself.

Learn about the culture associated with the language. This not only makes learning more interesting but also helps you understand the nuances of the language and enjoy your journey to Advanced English.

―――――――――――――――――― The End ――――――――――――――――――